LEIGH LINLEY

GREAT

YORKSHIRE

BOTTLED BEER

TRADITIONAL FAVOURITES
MODERN CLASSICS

GREAT NORTHERN

Great Northern Books

PO Box 213, Ilkley, LS29 9WS

www.greatnorthernbooks.co.uk

ISBN: 978-0-9928193-6-1

Design and layout: David Burrill

CIP Data

A catalogue for this book is available from the British Library

Acknowledgements

As with most guides, this book is truly a collaborative effort. I'd like to thank all the breweries involved for getting behind the project and giving up their time to talk to me. I'd also like to thank the team at Great Northern Books for again dipping their toe into the world of Yorkshire beer, and you, the reader, for picking this book up.

All brewery artwork reproduced with permission of the brewery involved. All photography by the author unless stated.

Specific Picture Credits: Spices – Tammy Luna; Brewing Diagram – Jamie Linley; Bad Seed Brewery Pictures – Victoria Harley (www.split-pin.co.uk); Picture of Malt, introduction – Great Newsome Brewery/Muntons; Picture of Hops, Yorkshire Squares/Fermentation, introduction – Black Sheep Brewery; Further Hops and water images released under Creative Commons.

About the author

Leigh Linley lives in Leeds with his family, which includes Wilson the border terrier, who has more fans than he does. He's been writing about beer since 2007 on his popular blog *The Good Stuff*, and his work has appeared in *Leeds Guide*, *Beer Magazine* and *The 100 Best Breweries in the World*, amongst others. He's also the author of the award-winning *Great Yorkshire Beer*, published by Great Northern Books in 2013.

Contents

Tasting Notes

Intro

One of the defining influences in my leap from 'I'm kind of curious about beer' to 'I want to taste every beer I can find!' was an early beer guide written by Michael Jackson - who was, of course, a fellow Yorkshireman - that I picked up in Oxfam in Headingley for less than the price of a pint.

It was a dense book (almost intimidatingly so) and packed with pictures of thirst-inducing glasses of beer that were as exotic-sounding as they were delicious-looking. Michael's loving descriptions of those beers – speaking about them as if they were old friends rather than simply glasses of liquid - did more than simply whet the appetite. It was pure inspiration; I pored over it, resolving to do my best to track down those beers. I'm still looking for some of them, and that endless quest for new tastes is what started my love affair with beer.

Drinking at home is part of modern life. Pubs are a deeply loved part of our personal history; be it warming up in that seat by the fire after an autumn country walk, restorative pint in hand - or sitting in shorts in a beer garden, swatting troublesome wasps away from a bittersweet pint of Pale ale. But we can't always be there. Sometimes your beer is one to take the edge off a busy day at work, pulled from the fridge and drunk straight from the bottle; sometimes it's an ice-bucket full of summer ales to wash down your Barbecue.

Bottled beer is a fantastic gift; a taste of a place. If you can't go to the beer - bring it to you. Buying a few from the same brewery gives you - in one session - a feel for what they are about, their 'house style', so to speak.

Whilst working on *Great Yorkshire Beer* in 2011 it became clear that people (drinkers, writers, brewers and publicans) were immensely proud of Yorkshire Beer. And I'm not just talking about their own wares - *but all of it*. We were Yorkshire, and we wanted our own space on the bookshelf.

So, the concept of this guide came to pass. Sure, there are plenty of bottled beer guides on the market, but hey - this one's ours. If someone picks it up and their interest is piqued in the same way that Michael Jackson's pictures and words did mine, then I think we've achieved what we set out to do.

A note on inclusion

I've tried my hardest to feature the most complete range of brewers and bottled beer produced in our fair county in this book as I can. I've also chosen beers that are readily available and regularly produced at the time of writing (i.e. not limited or special editions) in order to enhance the book's usefulness as a guide.

Leigh Linley, 2014.

So - what is beer, exactly?

All beers are made from the same raw ingredients – Water, Malt, Hops and Yeast. What makes each one different is the types of ingredients used, quantities of, and that magic factor: the brewer making it. Let's take a look at what we do in Yorkshire.

Water

One of the interesting things about water – which makes up most of that pint you've just poured – is that it's so varied in taste and composition. After all, many world-famous brewing centres such as Dublin and Burton upon Trent were built in those locations due to qualities of the waters that flowed there. As Yorkshire is such a big county, there's a little variance in the type of water brewers in the region receive; Ilkley, Harrogate and Sheffield's water is generally 'soft', whereas Masham, Leeds, York and Tadcaster are on the harder side. Regardless, you have to have good water to start with – and Yorkshire's is certainly excellent.

Some breweries, such as Timothy Taylor, Wentworth, Wold Top and Samuel Smith use water from their own wells and extract the spring-water directly, treating it as they wish to suit the style of beer they are brewing. Brewers refer to water as 'Liquor.'

Malt

Malted barley (or Malt) gives us the first sip we take of a beer; the one that draws your eye as you fill your glass. From shimmering golden ales to stout as black as Whitby jet, it's the blend of malted barley - and occasionally other grains – that gives us the diverse range of colour found in your bottle of beer.

Not only that, but malt provides the sugars that the yeast eats and turns into alcohol - as well as body. It's all simply down to the starches and sugars in the grain itself, which are released during the 'mash'. Mashing is simply steeping your grains in hot water, and the resultant liquid is called 'Wort'. It doesn't sound too nice, but that's the sweet base of your beer.

Malt is Barley that has been germinated, had the germination halted at precisely the right time, then kilned at varying temperatures. These degrees of roast impart different flavour and colour to the malt. It's then up to the brewer to mix and blend different types until they get the right colour and flavour for their beer.

Popular base malts such as Golden Promise and Maris Otter are often used on their own to produce a clean, pale beer; whereas adding Amber and Crystal malts will add degrees of caramel flavours and ruby hues to the beer. Intensely-roasted black malts do what they say on the tin in terms of colour, although dark beers (such as stout and porter) will only have a certain percentage of black malt, such is the powerful roast-profile of these grains.

Other grains are used too, adding further flavour, colour and body dimensions. Wheat, for example, promotes a smooth body and also helps produce that attractive frothy head on top of your pint. Subtly spicy Rye is popular, and Oats –

which add a silky, comforting sweetness to darker beers in particular – are widely used. Maize pops up in gluten-free beers.

Yorkshire and the Humber's malted barley is shipped all over the world, and nationally-known maltsters Muntons and Thomas Fawcett operate out of Bridlington and Castleford respectively.

Hops

People who are interested in beer often have favourite hops (mine are Cascade, Amarillo and Bramling Cross, if you're asking!) and it's easy to see why; hops lend character and personality to your favourite beer, whether it's in the nose - pulling you into the glass with fruit, flower, herbal or earthy aromas – or in the finish, giving bitterness that puckers the lips and implores you take another sip. Hop bines crawl up trellis supports, are nurtured, then picked as whole flowers or crushed into pellets before being sold to brewers in perfect condition. They're added to the wort at various stages of the boil and in different quantities - depending on what effect you want them to have. Beers such as mild and brown ale are traditionally hopped only lightly, whilst IPA's and strong pale ales are packed with hops.

The UK hop-growing industry is traditionally based in the south of England, although Yorkshire Hops have become Yorkshire's first Hop farmers, growing on a small scale on their farm in Ellerker, near Hull. Saltaire, Great Newsome and Ossett are a few of the brewers who have recently brewed with Yorkshire Hops.

Yeast

A brewer may tell you what malt and hops go into his beer – but will be coy when it comes yeast. With good reason, too; yeast doesn't just eat the sugars in the wort and then expel alcohol (along with carbon dioxide) into the beer, it imparts flavours and aromas unique to that strain, too. Brewers use different strains of yeast to brew different styles of beer; Wheat and Saison beers, for example, all require specific strains of yeast to be brewed correctly. Lager also requires its own yeast (which is bottom-fermenting) in order to get that clean taste we love – one which enjoys a much cooler fermenting temperature than the regular temperature range that top-fermenting yeast (used in ale and beer) needs.

Traditionally, Yorkshire yeast – made famous by the likes of Tetley's, Samuel Smith and Black Sheep – has well-balanced, bready aroma and flavour profile that lets the malt's flavour shine through the beer unhindered, leaning toward a dry finish.

Wait...there's more?

Yes! Although the above ingredients are what gives us the beers we know and love, brewers add little treats along the way to either create new flavours or twist existing styles. Vanilla, coffee, chocolate, cinnamon, star anise, chilli, herbs, honey and maple syrup, pepper, fruit, pumpkin and even tea-leaves are among the cornucopia of extra flavours added to beer to give drinkers new flavours to enjoy.

Right; here's how beer is brewed – broadly speaking!

Yorkshire water is heated (1) and then blended with crushed malt (2) as it's poured into the mash tun (3), where the resultant mixture steeps. The run-off from this – called wort – is then boiled (4) in the copper (or kettle) and has hops added to it during that boiling period. The wort is then pushed through a whirlpool (5) to remove debris and spent hops before being cooled (6). Yeast is added to the wort in the fermentation vessel (7), and once fermentation is complete, it's conditioned (8) for a while before finally being bottled.

Then it's just up to you to buy it, pour it – and enjoy it!

Beer Styles

There are loads of recognised beer styles in the world - and to make things a little more complex (or interesting, depending on your viewpoint!), many brewers happily mix the styles together to create hybrids from time to time. Here's some examples of what you should expect from the major beer styles - and a little pointer in terms of what foods generally go well with them. Whether you want something easy-going and 'sessionable' whilst watching the football game, or a rich, comfortingly complex beer to be savoured and sipped, there's a beer style for you.

Bitter/ESB

Bitter may be a term that conjures up beer from a bygone age but, rest assured, it still exists - and a well-brewed bitter is still a thing of beauty. This classic British beer style focuses on sheer drinkability, so expect mild, sweet flavours such as creamy toffee, biscuit and toasted brown bread in the body. You can also taste a little dash of fruitiness - recalling sultana or raisin – in some darker examples. Aroma-wise, you're getting more biscuit, some nuttiness, or pungent floral notes. Alcohol is usually low to moderate, although bitterness can be relatively high - considering the sweetness of the beer

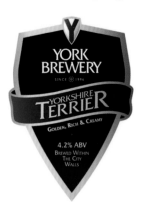

itself. Colour is usually bright, brassy copper although some (such as Timothy Taylor's Landlord and Theakston Best) are positively golden. Best Bitter, 'Amber Ale' and ESB (Extra Strong/Special Bitter) are offshoots of this style.

Classic Examples: *Black Sheep Best Bitter, Sam Smiths Old Brewery Bitter, Ilkley Joshua Jane, Acorn Barnsley Bitter, York Yorkshire Terrier.*

What to Eat: Earthy, honest Bitter needs earthy and honest food, so don't overcomplicate things here – pork pies and sweet chutney, Ploughman's platters, grilled steak and mushrooms, scotch eggs and rarebit all love a pint of Bitter.

Pale Ale

One of the widest-used terms in beer, Pale Ales are everywhere these days, appealing perhaps to a wider audience than bitter. Some of Yorkshire's Pale Ales are bona-fide classics, traditional in taste and history, whereas some of the newer ones look across the seas to America or New Zealand for inspiration. Typically, you're looking at a pale straw to golden-hued beer, with a light mouthfeel and a soft, creamy malt profile. Pale Ales should also have a sprightly aroma - ranging from floral, herbaceous notes to ripe tropical fruit, mango and citrus notes. Alcohol content can be diverse; generally speaking, Pale Ales are on the lower end of the spectrum, but Strong Pale ales (such as Wharfe Bank's SPA and Samuel Smith's Pale Ale) and US-inspired Pale ales ramp up the alcohol strength. Expect light, fresh and subtly spicy notes in both the body and aroma where Blonde ales are concerned.

Classic Examples: *Saltaire Cascade Pale Ale, Leeds Brewery Pale, Magic Rock Ringmaster, Ilkley Mary Jane, Copper Dragon Golden Pippin, Rooster's Yankee.*

What to Eat: Pale Ales sing with grilled or fried seafood - calamari, scampi or herbed lemon sole for example - as well as good old-fashioned fish and chips. Omelette and Spanish-style Tortilla (best eaten cold if you ask me) are good, too - and you can't go wrong with Quiche Lorraine or Grilled Vegetable Tart.

India Pale Ale

IPA is the style that's spearheaded the boom in "Craft Beer" and nurtured our modern love of hops - and Yorkshire is producing some real knockouts at the moment. A good IPA should have an aroma bursting with hop; whether that be woody, earthy, fruity notes, sappy, oily Pine, or explosions of tropical fruit and citrus - aroma is one of the key aspects drinkers look for in IPA. Another is body and alcohol; typically both should be robust and the beer should have a rolling, bitter finish. The best IPA's achieve harmony between creamy malt and vibrant hop; quenching thirst and leaving you gagging for another sip. Colour can range from amber to burnished copper in the glass - although Black IPA's (IPA brewed with darker malts to create an IPA with a richer, almost Porter-esque backbone) are also popular.

Classic Examples: *Rooster's Fort Smith, Kirkstall Dissolution IPA, Summer Wine Diablo, Magic Rock Cannonball, Little Valley Python IPA, Samuel Smith's India Ale.*

What to Eat: IPA can stand up to rich, powerfully flavoured foods - so think along the lines of Tandoori chicken wings, chilli nachos and grilled peppers stuffed with goat's cheese. You can also go for some sweetness, too - sliced pineapple and mango, glazed with honey and grilled is a different, explosively fruity accompaniment for IPA. I can't resist it with a slice of piquant pepperoni pizza!

Stout

Pitch-black in hue and with a low hop profile, a pint of Stout is a comforting embrace of sweetness and smoke. Creamy yet bittersweet to taste, Stout should have a dry, bitter finish overlaid with chocolate, wood-smoke and coffee notes. Again, the range of versions is staggering - from strong Imperial Stout and wood-aged versions to milk, oatmeal and chocolate stouts. Expect regular  stouts to be easy-going in terms of alcohol.

Classic Examples: *Brass Castle Bad Kitty, Great Newsome Gem's Stout, Acorn Gorlovka, Black Sheep Russian Imperial Stout, Rudgate York Chocolate Stout.*

What to Eat: Stout is not only perfect with Oysters and Prawn Cocktail (really!), but with desserts, too. Vanilla Cheesecake, Yorkshire Parkin and Black Forest Gateau all work well, as does Hazelnut Torte... oh, and a glass of plain old vanilla ice-cream. Plonk a dollop in your glass and top with shaved chocolate for an indulgent Vanilla Ice Cream Stout Float. My favourite, however, is a slice of intensely salty blue cheese – a match made in heaven.

Porter

Stylistically and historically related to Stout (some say the two are more or less the same beer), Yorkshire's Porters tend to be a little lighter and fruitier in flavour than Stout. There's sometimes a burst of black cherry or raisin lurking in the middle, and Porters tend to finish a little sweeter.

Porter, when held to the light, can often reveal a ruby streak running through them. Again, the nose should be full of woodsmoke, bready malt and light coffee notes.

Classic Examples: *Acorn Old Moor Porter, Elland 1872, Summer Wine Teleporter, Revolutions Clash London Porter, Roosters Londinium.*

What to Eat: Air-cured Beef (Bresaola), Raisin Loaf, lightly spiced sausage (such as Boerewors) and Cherry Pie are all complemented wonderfully with a glass of silky, smooth Porter.

Wheat & Wit

Wheat Beers are terrifically thirst-quenching and the light malt profile offers a massive potential for experimentation. Varying in colour from pale straw to amber, expect a generously abundant white head to stick your nose into and enjoy those wonderful aromas billowing forth. Banana, bubblegum, cereal and even spices like pepper and clove can be found - courtesy of the type of yeast used in these kinds of beers. To complement the aroma, Wheat beers should have a sweet mouthfeel, and appear naturally hazy – although you can get clear versions, too. Expect a drying, albeit fruity, finish. Dark Wheat (Dunkelweisse) beers add a little woodsmoke and light coffee note to proceedings, and have a drier finish.

Wit Beer - a typically Belgian or Dutch variant of Wheat beer - also adds Orange Peel and other Citrus notes to give a sharper, more acidic finish.

Classic Examples: *Magic Rock Clown Juice, Bad Seed Hefewiezen, Five Towns Schneider V2, Little Valley Hebden's Wheat, Great Heck Amish Mash.*

What to Eat: Wheat beer is brilliant with banoffee pie - the two share so many flavours. Fried fish and fiery vegetable bhaji are perfect partners, too. I also enjoy wheat beer with mild, creamy curries such as Thai green or Korma - they offer so much more flavour than lager yet remain light, refreshing the palate immensely. Truthfully, though, there's not much Wheat Beer doesn't go with - it's hugely versatile.

Saison

Interest in the Saison style has exploded in recent years, and with good reason – if you like Wheat or Wit beers, you'll find plenty of interest here. Saisons originated in Wallonia (French-speaking Belgium), brewed to quench thirsts of workers in the fields. Brewed with pale malt, they can vary wildly in flavour and feel, but typically expect a refreshing beer with a bright, golden hue and a tart, acidic finish with plenty of grassy hop aroma. On the nose, there's some similar notes as you'd find in wheat beer (including spice such as coriander and white pepper) as well as herbal notes such as thyme and rosemary. It's not uncommon to find hybrids on the shelves, either, such as IPA or Pale Ales brewed with Saison yeast to inject a wild, earthy character into the base beer.

Classic Examples: *Ilkley Siberia, Bad Seed Saison.*

What to Eat: Barbecued, herbed chicken and lemon meringue pie are two matches that you perhaps wouldn't immediately think of for Saison but work well. Smoked fish such as Salmon or Trout are lifted gently by the citrus side of Saison - and consider one alongside a platter of medium-hard cheese, cured meats and sharp, tangy pickles.

Lager

The term Lager, loosely, means "to store" - which refers to the cold maturation that Lager undergoes in order to, well, become Lager. The style also has offshoots: expect Vienna lagers to be darker and toastier in body and Helles to be on the lighter end of colour and flavour. Yorkshire does have a handful of popular lagers – they've been included in the main body of the book.

Classic Examples: *Sam Smith's Pure Brewed Lager.*

What to Eat: Lager is so light and easy-going that your mind immediately turns to summery food – grilled prawns, baked salmon with dill and char-grilled peppers. It's also pretty adept at cutting through softer cheeses such as Brie, believe it or not.

Strong & Old Ale, Barley Wine

Yorkshire has produced some world-class strong and old ales; intended as much for laying down and ageing as much as enjoying year-on-year to see what differences become apparent in this year's batch. There's a lot to choose from in terms of flavour (depending on the brewer's tastes) but typically you should expect complex vinous, robustly malt-led flavours (think Malt loaf, all sticky-sweet) in the body and warming aromas including tobacco, leather, cherry, rum and caramel notes in Old Ale – which should be deep ruby in hue. And, of course, a warming alcohol caress as you swallow.

Barley Wine can differ in colour from Golden to Brown, and again should display complex, sherry or port-esque characteristics, along with plenty of dried-fruit, grain-malt and biscuit tones, with a sweet finish and a powerful alcohol kick.

Classic Examples: *Theakston Old Peculier, Black Sheep Riggwelter, Sam Smith's Yorkshire Stingo*

What to Eat: Strong and Old Ales are wonderful enjoyed with cheeses - and can stand up to stronger aged or complex blue cheeses. Lamb's mild character dovetails nicely with old ales, enhancing the sweetness of the meat. Barley Wine is really intended to be sipped, but if you do want to enjoy something to eat too, try to complement the beer with dried fruits such as apricot and date - and perhaps even a good old Christmas Pudding?

Tasting Notes

Acorn Brewery

Dave Hughes started his brewing career at Barnsley Brewery, before setting up Acorn Brewery in Wombwell with his wife, Judi, in 2003. Using kit from a Firkin pub in Stafford - and their Barnsley Bitter as a flagship beer - Acorn quickly grew into a formidable regional brewer. They now have their own pub, too: The Old No 7, on Market Hill in Barnsley. Keep an eye out for Acorn's IPA range; the hops used rotate on a brew-by-brew basis.

www.acorn-brewery.co.uk 🐦 *@acornbrewery*

Barnsley Bitter

Style: **Bitter**

ABV: **3.8%**

A multiple award winner, Barnsley Bitter is a recreation of Barnsley Brewery's original beer of the same name. Crucially, Dave Hughes and his brewing partner, Steve Bunting, saw fit to make sure that they used some of the original yeast when they formulated the recipe. That yeast is the star here – Barnsley Bitter boasts a nutty, caramel-sweet nature but it comes alive in the distinctive aroma; peppery and doughy with fresh bread. The finish is short and dry. A classic example of Yorkshire Bitter.

Old Moor Porter

Style: **Porter**

ABV: **4.4**%

Named after the nearby Old Moor wetlands, this popular dark ruby porter packs heaps of flavour into a relatively low-strength package. The nose carries molasses and smoky roasted malt aroma, both of which pop up in the taste alongside bittersweet Pontefract cake. Mild, mellow coffee dries out the finish, making Old Moor Porter a very seductive beer indeed.

Gorlovka Imperial Stout

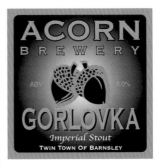

Style: **Imperial Stout**

ABV: **6%**

Gorlovka, Barnsley's Ukrainian twin town, is honoured with this beast of an imperial stout. Coal-black and thick on both the tongue and the glass, Gorlovka's aroma begs contemplation; wafer, bitter chocolate, woodsmoke and a bramble fruitiness all climbing out of the glass. Silky-smooth and loaded with bitter Bournville chocolate, the dry finish rises in intensity to wash the sweetness away to a soporific climax that's spiritous with alcohol. Majestic and complex.

Ampleforth Abbey

Ampleforth Abbey Beer is one of Yorkshire's best kept secrets. Created by brewer Wim Van Der Spek (Little Valley Brewery) and Father Wulstan Peterburs of Ampleforth Abbey in North Yorkshire after researching monastic beer in the Netherlands and Belgium's low countries, their interpretation of the style revives the brewing tradition of the English Benedictines settled in France. Now produced regularly, it's sold widely as well as directly from Ampleforth alongside their own ciders and brandies. As you can imagine, it's a wonderful partner to cheeses and roasted dark meats – beef, in particular.

www.visitors.ampleforth.org.uk 🐦 *@AmplerforthBeer*

Ampleforth Abbey Double/Dubbel

Style: **Dubbel**

ABV: **7%**

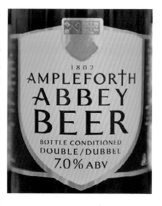

Blending Pale, Wheat Chocolate, Crystal and Munich malts, Ampleforth Double pours a dark mahogany, revealing a ruby streak within when held to the light. The nose is dominated by bready malt, spicy yeast and sweet vine fruit, all of which appear in the body alongside touches of nutmeg, tangy sultana and rich brown sugar. The beer remains light thanks to a subtle carbonation which lifts all the sweetness from the tongue and helps build to the slightly sour finish. The alcoholic strength becomes apparent after the sip, although Ampleforth Dubbel remains an incredibly approachable beer.

Atom Brewery

It was the science of brewing and the manipulation of flavour that drove 'Chief Beer Geek' Allan Rice and Sarah Thackray to set up Atom Brewery in 2013. Indulging their mutual love of experimentation, the Beverley-based duo have already created un-hopped beers, collaborated with coffee-roasters and other brewers, as well as thrusting their beer into the hands of drinkers in cask, keg and bottle in less than a year. With that work ethic, I suspect you'll be seeing Atom's wares pretty much everywhere by the time you read this!

www.atombeers.com 🐦 *@atombeers*

Pale Ale

Style: **Pale Ale**

ABV: **4.5%**

Simply named and simply delicious, Atom's Pale Ale ticks all the boxes if it's a vivacious, golden Pale ale with a sweet, smooth body and subtly aromatic nose you're after. Interestingly, Atom don't ascribe to one particular hop with this beer's recipe; it'll change depending simply on what's the best when they brew it. My sample was hopped with the green, oily pine and gloriously grapefruit personalities of Cascade and Chinook.

Dark Alchemy

Style: **Porter**

ABV: **4.9%**

As you've probably gathered, Atom like to do things a little differently and, given that they like to enjoy Porter with spicy food, decided to brew an un-hopped one so they could use spice additions for aroma and bitterness. A silky body laden with cappuccino coffee and milk chocolate is overlaid with an aroma of spiky stem ginger; the complex, sweet finish is where the additions of cardamom and coriander come into play. It's a beer that brings out richness in red meat - I enjoyed mine with some Nachos loaded with piquant beef chilli.

Bunsen

Style: **Brown Ale**

ABV: **5.1%**

It's an interesting beer, this: an American-inspired brown ale matured on chestnuts. Darker and markedly hoppier than a British brown ale, Bunsen pours a lovely autumnal brown and boasts an aroma that balances fresh, peppery hop with wholemeal toast. There's an attractive tan head, and the mouthfeel is thick and sweet: hazelnut, bran flake and bonfire toffee all compete for attention in the flavour. The finish, however, is fresh and crisp - balancing out all that chewy, wholesome nut in the body.

Bad Seed Brewery

"All great adventures start with a bad seed of an idea…" say Chris Waplington and James Broad, the youthful duo who turned their idea into reality and created Bad Seed Brewery in 2013. The Malton-based brewery have enjoyed critical success from the start; particularly adept at interpreting continental beer styles, their simply-named, brightly-labelled beers with hand-printed tags are easy to spot on the shelf. They - along with neighbours Brass Castle Brewery - are also behind Beer Town, Malton's independent beer festival.

www.badseedbrewery.com 🐦 *@badseedbrewery*

Hefeweizen

Style: **Wheat Beer**

ABV: **5.1**

Take in that aroma before you sip; cedar wood, a little coriander and ginger zing, and a touch of bubblegum abound beneath that billowing white head. This wheat beer may pack a decent punch in terms of alcohol but you can't tell - such is the light, sweetly spritzy feel to the beer: it glides across the tongue leaving a sweet finish with a lemon-led spark to liven things up. Serve slightly chilled.

Saison

Style: **Saison**

ABV: **6%**

With a complex, yeasty aroma that takes in creamy malt and vanilla, peppercorn, freshly-sliced ginger and lemongrass, this golden Saison has an incredibly smooth, rounded mouthfeel with plenty of wildflower honey and a finish that brings to mind lime preserve; sharp and biting, yet refreshingly citric. A supple, refreshing beer that serves well a little chilled.

Espresso Stout

Style: **Stout**

ABV: **7%**

Hiding considerable alcoholic strength within its coal-black depths, Espresso Stout is the perfect gift for the coffee geeks in your life. Rich, roasted coffee bean dominates the nose, and although the body of the beer is thin, it's laden with more grainy coffee, a touch of black cherry, bitter dark chocolate and a touch of vanilla cream in the finish. There's real espresso clout in this stout.

Ben Rhydding Brewery

Steve Shaw made the leap from keen homebrewer to commercial brewer in 2010, inspired by a trip to Saltaire Brewery and travels with his day job that had exposed him to the beers of the USA and Germany. After a year of planning and converting his garage into a small brewery, he's now turning out his own tasty beer. His beers are all bottle-conditioned, and, although produced on a small scale, are well worth seeking out.

www.benrhyddingbrewery.co.uk 🐦 *@benrhyddingbrew*

Pale Ale 62

Style: **Pale Ale**

ABV: **4.8%**

A lower-strength version of the IPA's that showcase Steve's brewing style so well. Vibrant amber in hue, the body strikes a balance between firm biscuit and hard-candy gumminess. The hops are the star of the show here; the blend of Amarillo and Kohatu (a New Zealand native) gives us a fruit-salad aroma of lime, pineapple, tangerine and a sharp, lime-accented finish that's increasingly dry as it fades out.

IPA 63

Style: **IPA**

ABV: **6.7%**

Simply named and numbered but complex in flavour, this is a modern IPA that ticks all the boxes in today's hop-centric times. On top of the sticky, lip-smacking copper-coloured malt base sits an aroma that snaps with mango, Seville orange peel and lemon pith, lychee and juicy pineapple. Beginning incredibly sweet but then flipping to a resinous, biting finish, the hops used in this brew were Columbus, Centennial and Citra.

Black Sheep Brewery

You'd think Black Sheep have been around forever, such is their imprint on the beer landscape in Yorkshire. In reality, the brewery was famously set up in 1991 by Paul Theakston, whose family had been brewing in Masham for years. Black Sheep Brewery – named after Paul's attitude to brewing and also celebrating those famous residents of the surrounding countryside – set up in a maltings building that once belonged to the Lightfoot Brewery and begun brewing in earnest. The rest is history, and Black Sheep are now the first thing a beer hunter thinks of when they think of Masham.

www.blacksheepbrewery.com 🐦 *@BlackSheepBeer*

All Creatures

Style: **Pale Ale**

ABV: **4%**

The newest bottled beer of Black Sheep's family, All Creatures (named to celebrate the works of Alf Wight who, under the pen name of James Herriot, created the *All Creatures Great and Small* stories), is a bright, golden pale ale with a nimble, light biscuit flavour and a fresh, almost floral finish laced with just a hint of citrus fruit.

Black Sheep Ale

Style: **Bitter**

ABV: **4.4%**

The daddy of the family. This multiple award-winning beer still packs a bitter punch; that long, risingly dry finish is powered by Goldings hops. Deep amber in colour, the nose of the beer evokes bready, fruity yeast and both the sip and the finish is juicily bittersweet. Full-flavoured yet rounded in taste, Black Sheep Ale is a true Yorkshire classic; balanced yet forthright in attitude.

Riggwelter

Style: **Strong/Old Ale**

ABV: **5.7%**

When a sheep has rolled onto its back and cannot right itself, it's said to be 'Rigwelted'; one too many bottles of this powerful ruby beer will have the same effect. Astoundingly complex and boasting a luxuriously tan head, Riggwelter's aroma boasts a vinous nose; all wood and plummy dark fruit with an interesting whisper of banana in the background. The smooth, slick body of the beer – sweet with brown sugar, liquorice and a little molasses – fills the mouth and leaves a dry, roasted coffee note in its wake. Try adding a splash to a beef or lamb casserole to add a little depth.

Bobage Brewery

By day, Sarah and Jason Salvin run an events management company; by night they are Bobage Brewery, producing small runs of bottled beer for the entertainment industry - alongside the odd cask or two here and there – out of their tiny brewery in Leeds. Although I've featured only one of their beers here, keep an eye out for the Wilson's Vintage Green, which is brewed with fresh hops from Yorkshire.

www.bobagebrewery.co.uk 🐦 *@bobagebrewing*

Wilson's Vintage No 1

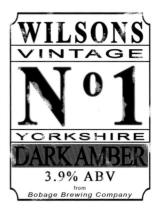

Style: **Bitter**

ABV: **3.9%**

Wilson's Vintage No 1 (named in honour of Jason's grandfather) pours a deep shade of mahogany and sees roasted malt and crisp hazelnut battling away in the aroma. A rich beer for its strength, the sweet, full body pairs intense nuttiness with fudgy toffee flavours, before topping things off with a powerfully dry finish peppered with wholemeal bread notes.

Bradfield Brewery

The Gill Family's farm in the hills of Bradfield may have been built on Dairy farming, but when they decided to diversify and brew beer as well, little did they know that their future lay in the art of blending malt and hop rather than milk. The brews were so successful that they devoted themselves solely to brewing, but ensure that their history lives on in their cheeky cow motif that adorns their labels and pumpclips.

www.bradfieldbrewery.co.uk 🐦 @BradfieldBrew

Farmer's Brown Cow

Style: **Bitter**

ABV: 4.2%

Perhaps the elder statesman of the herd, Brown Cow is a moreish, tasty bitter that satisfies. Deep chestnut in colour, the light, toffee and nut-accented body is spiced up with a spiky hop aroma with hints of black pepper. The finish is grainy and creamily sweet – echoes of Scottish tablet, perhaps?

Farmer's Stout

Style: **Stout**

ABV: **4.5%**

The Gills fondly refer to their stout as *black and white*, recalling the typical Friesian cow's hide markings. It's a loving description for a simple, creamy stout – all crushed chocolate digestives and sweet roasted barley in the body with a dry, bitter finish embellished with a little espresso coffee.

Farmer's Blonde

Style: **Blonde**

ABV: **4%**

One of Sheffield's best-selling beers, Farmer's Blonde has amassed loads of awards over the years. It's easy to see why; this brilliantly pale, refreshing beer with a twist of lemon and orange in the finish is supremely sessionable. The cow on the label is a Blonde d'Aquitaine, a French breed known for their light tan-coloured hides. A sister beer, if you will, to Farmer's Brown Cow.

Brass Castle Brewery

Phil Saltonstall – the ex-RAF Coastguard behind Brass Castle – set up Brass Castle Brewery in Pocklington in 2011 after cutting his teeth brewing in America during a period of relocation. Launching with the instantly-popular *Bad Kitty Vanilla Porter*, success soon followed and in 2013 they relocated to nearby Malton. Bold as brass in flavour, Brass Castle's beer are all Vegan friendly.

www.brasscastlebrewery.co.uk 🐦 @BrassCastleBeer

Bad Kitty

Style: **Stout**

ABV: **5.5%**

Bad Kitty is one Vanilla stout that will have you purring. Yes, the aroma is pleasantly creamy – all vanilla pod and oak – but there's an intriguing touch of blackcurrant bobbing along behind it that stops the beer from being too cloying or sweet. That dark fruit and creamy chocolate mix – not unlike a Black Forest Gateaux, actually – carries on into the body, before drying up in the finish. A deserved multiple-award winner.

Brass Lager

Style: **Lager**

ABV: **5.3%**

You may be shocked if you're expecting a frothy, golden pilsner here. Brass Lager is a lager in the Vienna style and therefore all about the malt. Copper (well, *brassy*, actually) in hue and boasting a fulsome body of nutty, wholemeal bread, *just a smidge* of gingerbread from the yeast, and a crisp, flinty finish.

Sunshine IPA

Style: **IPA**

ABV: **5.7**

If you can take a sip of this beer without spending at least a minute simply sniffing it, you've got better willpower than me! This flame-coloured IPA worships at the altar of American West-Coast IPA and comes pretty close to transporting you there instantly; the aroma is uplifting, bristling with pungent mango, strawberry and jammy citrus. The mouthfeel is richly comforting with boiled-sweet thickness, before the real party begins with lime peel, more mango and lychee smoothing out the waspish, bracingly bitter finish.

Bridestones Brewing

The Bridestones are a sandstone rock formation that stand glowering on the edge of Stansfield Moor near Todmorden. The group of impressive stones – the focus of which is the upturned-bottle shaped "Bride" – provided the inspiration for Dan Tasker when he set up the brewery in 2006. Situated in Blackshaw Head, Bridestones Brewing's bottles are widely available, although The New Delight Inn in Hebden Bridge is a good place to catch their cask beers if you fancy a day out!

www.bridestonesbrewing.co.uk 🐦 *@BridestonesBeer*

Pennine Gold

Style: **Pale Ale**

ABV: **4.3%**

Bridestones' inaugural brew, Pennine Gold remains the most popular of Bridestones' beer range. Straw-gold and boasting a lightly citrus aroma (think lemon peel and apricot), this easy-going session beer has a heart of toasted malt and wheat, culminating in a softly bittersweet finish.

American Pale

Style: **Pale Ale**

ABV: **5%**

This stronger transatlantic cousin to Pennine Gold will satisfy those who like a more robust malt and hop profile to their pale ales. Seasoned with the popular Willamette hop, you've got an aroma that mixes fruit and flora; all summery orange pith and blackcurrant, undercut with a green herbaceous note. Gloriously amber in colour, the beer is thick in body, coating the tongue with smooth toasted malt which is quickly obliterated by belligerent hop bitterness of grapefruit and lemon sherbet. A long, dry finish readies you for the next sip.

Brown Cow Brewery (Simpson & Simpson)

Susan and Keith Simpson set up Brown Cow Brewery in Selby in 1997. Brewing a small-yet-perfectly-formed range of beers, Brown Cow's beers are always a welcome sight on bars across the region. Two beers in particular – Captain Oates Mild and Mrs Simpson's Vanilla Porter – are multiple award winners, proving that quality really does last.

www.browncowbrewery.co.uk

Captain Oates Mild

Style: **Mild**

ABV: **4.5%**

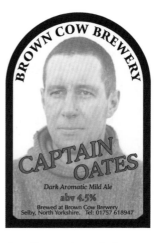

A deliciously sustaining dark mild that is one of Yorkshire's finest examples of the style. Topped with a creamy, tan head, the near-black ruby beer carries a nose of bitter chocolate, mild coffee and digestive biscuit notes. The body is smoothly sweet, balancing roasted malt flavour with almond nuttiness. The finish has more roasted malt and coffee notes, drying on the swallow. Try with a slice of Yorkshire Parkin for a mid-afternoon treat.

Mrs Simpson's Vanilla Porter

Style: **Porter**

ABV: **5.1%**

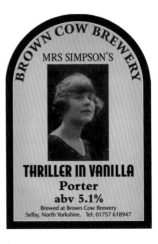

Punningly subtitled *'Thriller in Vanilla'*, Mrs Simpson's Vanilla Porter is as satisfying as the Captain Oates Mild - if not more so. Black in colour but with an almost purplish hue when held to the light, the nose is rich with cream, some oakiness, rum truffle and digestive-biscuit personality. Blackberry and cherry notes liven things up in the body and a dollop of cream at the finish enhances its flamboyant billing whilst remaining gracefully drinkable. A perennial crowd-pleaser for lovers of vanilla porter.

Copper Dragon Brewery

Steve Taylor and Ruth Bennett founded Copper Dragon Brewery in 2002, eager to bring brewing back to the historic market town. With a brewing team guided by master brewer Gordon Wilkinson, the success of beers such as Golden Pippin and Black Gold secured the brewery's reputation as one of Yorkshire's finest brewers. Copper Dragon's gleaming Bavarian-style brewery is well worth a visit - followed by lunch in their excellent Bistro, which is the perfect place to try all of their beers alongside top-notch food.

www.copperdragon.co.uk 🐦 *@CDBrewery*

Golden Pippin

Style: **Pale Ale**

ABV: **4.2**

Originally a seasonal summer beer, Golden Pippin was so popular upon its release in 2003 that the brewery had no choice but to brew it all year round. Now, this fresh, crisp pale ale – all lemon and lime in the aroma and distinct grapefruit bitterness in the finish - is one of Yorkshire's most popular beers; you won't find many pubs in Skipton that don't stock it.

Scott's 1816

Style: **Bitter**

ABV: **4.4%**

The "Scott" in question here is Christopher Scott, a maltster from Leeds who set up the original Skipton Brewery in 1816, unwittingly writing the first chapter in the story of brewing in Skipton that Copper Dragon now continue. Scott's 1816 is a classic Yorkshire bitter; rye bread and fruitloaf in the nose, smooth and sweet with malt-loaf and a little cinnamon spice in the body, and a crisp snap of hop at the finish.

Black Gold

Style: **Dark Mild**

ABV: **3.7%**

Black Gold is an apt name – a good bottled dark mild can be a rare beast in today's hop-centric climate. Copper Dragon have certainly kept up tradition with Black Gold, which is the perfect partner to one of the huge steaks served in the bistro. Expect a smoky, grainy nose, underpinned by a little treacle toffee and a body that adds a light, fruity sultana touch to proceedings. The gently sweet finish brings the curtain down with just a touch of drying coffee, cocoa and a whisper of woodsmoke.

Cropton Brewery

Cropton Brewery has been brewing fine ales since 1984, reviving a brewing tradition in the village that goes back as early as 1613. Famously starting life at The New Inn in Pickering, the brewing operation soon moved to its own building just behind the pub - all thanks to the success of their flagship bitter, *Two Pints*. Now visitors flock to The New Inn to sample the home-cooked food, surrounding landscape and – of course – Cropton's delicious, full-flavoured beers. Cropton's beers are still available, despite their recent rebranding as *The Great Yorkshire Brewery* (see later entry).

www.croptonbrewery.com 🐦 *@yorkshirebeer*

Yorkshire Warrior

Style: **Bitter**

ABV: **4.4%**

Brewed to honour the efforts of the Yorkshire Regiment, Yorkshire Warrior is a fittingly hearty, rich bitter that's a wonderful partner to stews and roasted meat. Ruby in colour, Yorkshire Warrior carries an aroma of fudge, date and a comforting bready note, whilst the taste of the beer brings more caramel to the fore alongside a fruity dark berry note. Only moderate in bitterness, the finish is dry with a touch of brown sugar.

Yorkshire Moors

Style: **Bitter**

ABV: **4.6%**

Brewed to commemorate 50 years of the North Yorkshire National Park, Yorkshire Moors is another steadfast mahogany bitter from Cropton, although lighter in flavour than Yorkshire Warrior. Nutty, cookie-esque aroma abounds and is backed up by Demerara sugar and earthy malt; the finish crisp and fleetingly dry. Hopped with Fuggle and Progress hops.

Monkman's Slaughter

Style: **Strong/Old Ale**

ABV: **6%**

This beer doesn't tell the story of a gruesome massacre; it's just a tribute to Cropton's malt farmer, Colin Monkman, and their brewer, Colin Slaughter. I would imagine they'd have been pleased at tasting this pleasantly soporific strong beer; sultana and raisin in the aroma, Yorkshire parkin in the body - think allspice, toffee and ginger - and a thick, bittersweet finish with a satisfyingly boozy kick.

Daleside Brewery

Brewing for over 25 years, Daleside Brewery is very much a brewing institution in Harrogate. Head Brewer Craig Witty's elegant, flavoursome beers - such as Monkey Wrench, Morocco Ale and Blonde - have amassed a serious trophy haul over the years, as well as a loyal and faithful following. Daleside also run the fantastic beer festival at Leyburn's annual Festival of Food and Drink.

www.dalesidebrewery.co.uk 🐦 *@DalesideBrewery*

Ripon Jewel

Style: **Bitter**

ABV: **5.8%**

The "Ripon Jewel" is a Saxon brooch, discovered on the grounds of Ripon's glorious cathedral in 1976. Still on display, it also adorns the label of the amber beer Daleside brewed to honour it. The beer itself carries more than an air of the ecclesiastical; hearty and forthright in flavour and body, brimming with rich, deep raisin and honey flavours in the sip and aroma and finishing with a spiky, leafy bitterness.

Morocco Ale

Style: **Old Ale**

ABV: **5.5%**

As the name suggests, Morocco Ale isn't your average pint of Yorkshire bitter. Brewed using a recipe retained in the family at Levens Hall, Cumbria and used since the 16th Century, it honours Catherine of Braganza, King Charles II's wife. The recipe was passed to Daleside in 1995, who resurrected this enigmatic beer for the first time. The genius of it lies in its dainty personality; it's incredibly easy to drink despite all the flavours swirling around in it. Packing ginger, almond and black treacle into the aroma, and nutty, rich Yorkshire parkin flavours into the body, it finishes clean and sweet, before a hit of sherry-accented booze appears. An elegant, interesting beer.

Monkey Wrench

Style: **Strong Bitter**

ABV: **5.3%**

Unlike its swarthy sister Morocco Ale, there's nothing subtle about Monkey Wrench. Delicious as it is, it's a much more straight-ahead affair. Deep amber in hue, this strong ale shoves the malt to the front of the flavour; cereal, slightly woody and finishing with a little blackcurrant fruit to lift things a touch. Undeniably sweet, the aroma speaks of sultana and fruit cake, and the finish is short and dry.

Dark Horse Brewery

Although Dark Horse only bottle one beer, they've chosen one with real local clout. Richard and Carole Eyton-Jones set up Dark Horse Brewery in a converted barn in Hetton (near Skipton) in 2006. Although only a handful of beers are produced, Dark Horse rightly focus on *Hetton Pale Ale*, such is its popularity. You can find it - and a tasty best bitter – in pubs across North Yorkshire, with bottled Hetton going slightly further afield.

www.darkhorsebrewery.co.uk

Hetton Pale Ale

Style: **Pale Ale**

ABV: **4.2%**

This golden slice of Yorkshire heaven is brewed with water pulled up from the borehole on site at Hetton. With an aroma of wheaten malt underpinned by fragrantly floral hop and a clean, crisp finish, Hetton Pale Ale is a quintessential thirst-quenching pale ale. Simple in taste but utterly delicious, with every aspect of it's flavour perfectly defined.

Doncaster Brewery

Ian and Alison Blaylock realised a long-held ambition when they set up Doncaster Brewery in 2012. Ian – a mechanic by trade – typically built the brewery from scratch and, with a resolve to promote all that's good about Doncaster through his work, brewed his first brace of beers (*Sand House Blonde* and *Gold Cup*) in September that year. The brewery was later granted permission to use Doncaster's heraldic crest – you don't get a bigger stamp of approval than that.

www.doncasterbrewery.co.uk 🐦 *@DonnyBrewery*

Cheswold Bitter

Style: **Bitter**

ABV: **4.2%**

This chestnut brown bitter with a hazelnut aroma, malt loaf chewiness in the centre and toffee-led, sweet finish commemorates the "Cheswold" car, manufactured by E.W Jackson & Son in Doncaster between 1910 and 1914, which was named after the nearby river that branches off from the mighty Don. Very light for its strength, Cheswold Bitter is a lovely example of the style, and perfect as a post-work reviver.

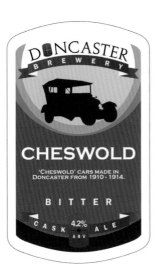

First Aviation

Style: **Pale Ale**

ABV: **5%**

In October 1909, Doncaster Racecourse held the first aviation meeting in England. With cash prizes and trophies supplied by (amongst others) The Daily Mail, the race actually set a new world record: Leon Delagrange completed the circuit in under two minutes. Doncaster Brewery's homage to that race is a strong pale ale; amber in colour and loaded with dominant biscuit flavour, topped off both in the aroma and dry finish with orange peel and cheeky grapefruit zing.

Elland Brewery

A Yorkshire brewing stalwart, Elland Brewery was founded as Eastwood and Sanders Fine Ales in 2002, bringing together the Barge and Barrel and West Yorkshire breweries. Gaining popularity with classic cask ales such as *Nettle Thrasher* and *Beyond the Pale*, the real award-winner in the portfolio is 1872 Porter, which was most recently named 'Champion Beer of Britain' by CAMRA in 2013.

www.ellandbrewery.co.uk 🐦 *@EllandBrewery*

1872 Porter

Style: **Porter**

ABV: **6.5%**

Garnet in hue when poured, 1872's brooding aroma brings to mind Port; notes of almond, tobacco and vine fruit issue from the glass, wrapped in chocolate and oaky woodsmoke. Black treacle, more dark chocolate and roasted grain smooth out the body of the beer, which is softly round on the palate, before finishing stoutly bittersweet to balance the soothing alcohol note that comes along at the end of the sip. Delightfully complex without overpowering your palate, 1872 Porter is based on a recipe dating from the same year, and is a true Victorian gent of a porter.

Firestorm Brewing Co

Before becoming head brewer at Wharfe Bank Brewery, Steve Crump was an award-winning homebrewer. He's kept the more experimental side of his talents going with Firestorm Brewing Co, which he produces at Wharfe Bank, but gives him another avenue to explore his brewing progression. Influenced by modern tastes, Firestorm's beers are available in keg as well as bottle.

http: www.firestorm-brewing.co 🐦 *@Firestormbeer*

Red Angel

Style: **Amber Ale**

ABV: **5%**

Red Angel certainly is that; pouring a deep, lusty crimson and boasting a heavenly aroma of fresh, floral hop underscored by sweet brown sugar. The sip is smooth and balanced despite its inherent sweetness – a little roasted malt and a touch of maple syrup, finishing with drying notes of Demerara sugar and bitter hop resins. A beer that drinks incredibly well for its strength, and is crying out for a fully-loaded, juicy burger to team up with.

Phoenix Pacific Pale Ale

Style: **Pale Ale**

ABV: **5.5%**

This laid-back golden pale ale manages to be both hearty and refreshing. With a creamy, full-bodied malt profile that gives depth to the lively, sassy citrus hop finish, Phoenix is another incredibly easy-to-drink beer from the Firestorm stable. Try this with some steamed and lightly-spiced prawns and clams, or a refreshing Greek Salad, covered in crumbled Feta cheese.

Fang

Style: **Stout**

ABV: **7%**

The alcohol content here firmly pushes Fang into 'Imperial' territory, but this brute doesn't bite. Expect a heavyweight nose boasting leather, tobacco, raisin and almond, all billowing from an incredibly attractive coffee-shaded head. On the sip, roasted malts and oak notes appear alongside a smooth coffee-and-cream streak. At the finish, a handful of blackcurrants and a smack of liquorice livens things up.

Five Towns Brewery

Malcolm Bastow's beers have gained somewhat of a cult following since he set up his bespoke brewery at the bottom of his garden in 2008. After years of praise, he finally began to bottle beer in 2012 and his bottled output is proving to be just as popular. Five Towns' beers are robust and full of flavour, and the monthly seasonals often take a walk on the wild side. The "five towns" in question are the provinces of Normanton, Pontefract, Castleford, Featherstone and Knottingley, in case you're wondering.

www.five-towns-brewery.blogspot.co.uk 🐦 *@FBrewery*

V2 Schneider

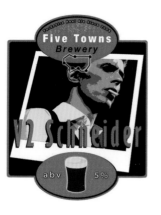

Style: **Dunkel** (Dark Wheat)

ABV: **6.2%**

You don't see bottled Dunkels much in Yorkshire, which is all the more reason to grab this Teutonic gem when you see it. V2 is deep brown in colour and pours with a tan-shaded, rocky head. The nose is wonderful; alive with banana, clove and raisin - as you'd want from a Dunkel. On the sip it's even more complex; hints of oak, some sour cherry, a touch of almond - even a little hint of Cola. It's seriously good stuff; one of my favourites in this guide.

Mango Junction

Style: **IPA**

ABV: **6%**

Ok, ok - I'll get it out of the way first. This fruity IPA does taste of Mango, you'll be relieved to know. Fruit IPA? Yeah, why not! Like all good IPA's, Mango Junction manages to be both refreshing and powerful; pouring burnished gold and brimming with the jammy,

fruity aroma of mango, strawberry and kiwi fruit. The flavour is initially sweet and fruity, but as the sip disappears down your throat a welcome bitterness kicks in - giving the beer a long, dry finish which seems to go on forever. There's nothing left to do but take another sip, of course - just to make sure.

Outwood Dark

Style: **Black IPA**

ABV: **3.9**

You may be thinking that Outwood Dark seems a little on the weak side for an IPA, but make no mistake: if you like IPA, then don't miss out on this gem. Combining explosive aroma – all yielding peach flesh, lychee, mango and sweet pineapple – with a soothing, soft roasted malt profile is the order

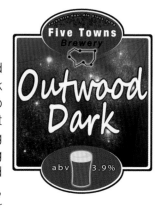

of the day here. A richly rewarding beer, Outwood Dark's low alcohol content proves to be the ace up its sleeve – it's a rousing, hop-filled ruby-dark beer that you can return to again and again without tiring the palate.

Geeves Brewery

The Geeves family's brewing history began in Worcestershire, rather than Yorkshire. And, uniquely, on a canal boat. Peter Geeves – an actor, whose work you can look up when you read this – experimented with brewing whilst living on the canal and, realising he had another talent beyond the stage, moved the family to Yorkshire to set up Geeves Brewery in 2011. The Geeves Brewery is now housed in Barnsley (where Peter had lived when studying) where the family brew their canal-themed beers for the masses. Oh, and if you're wondering what happened to the boat, it was sold to fund the brewery!

www.geevesbrewery.co.uk 🐦 @GeevesBrewery

Smokey Joe

Style: **Stout**

ABV: **5%**

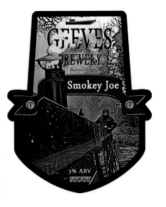

A "Smokey Joe" is the affectionate term for the wood-burning stove used on the canal boats to provide warmth, and this black-hearted little stout certainly lives up to that billing. Black as coal, and with a comforting aroma of bonfire toffee with a subtle woodsmoke undercurrent, Smokey Joe rolls across the tongue with roasted malt, creamy chocolate before wrapping things up with a fruity, liquorice-accented finish.

Fully Laden IPA

Style: **IPA**

ABV: **6%**

Pouring amber, Fully Laden IPA's nose is dominated by sweet fruit; think along the lines of candied orange peel and boiled sweets, and you're halfway there. The mouthfeel is sweeter still, rounded and smooth with a resinous hop attack as it finishes – more bitter orange pulp, some light tangerine, and only fleetingly dry.

Red Diesel

Style: **Bitter**

ABV: **4.1%**

As the name suggests, this beer pours a lush dark ruby colour and immediately fills the glass with a floral, spicy aroma that perfectly complements the layered malt flavour in the body; toffee, pecan nut, dense brown sugar and toasted wholemeal bread. The brisk, juicy finish makes Red Diesel a moreish and harmoniously balanced beer.

Goose Eye Brewery

There's been a Goose Eye Brewery at Ingrow for a while now: brewing initially began at The Turkey Inn in 1978. The brewery was revived by the Atkinson family in the early nineties, and they've continued to brew tasty ales for the residents of Bronte country. Goose Eye brew a full cask range, but only brew one beer for bottle, which is featured here.

www.goose-eye-brewery.co.uk 🐦 *@gooseeyebrewery*

Wonkey Donkey

Style: **Pale Ale**

ABV: **4.3%**

Despite the donkey on the label looking decidedly worse for wear, Wonkey Donkey is really a very easy-going pale ale. This straw-coloured beer's aroma is subtly herbal, and the beer itself softly fruity; bittersweet, rather than dry.

Great Heck Brewing Company

Selby's Great Heck Brewery – the brainchild of self-styled 'Supreme Overlord' Denzil Vallance - has grown from cult status to regional favourite with a pack of idiosyncratic beers that range from sweet-natured session beers such as *Dave* and *Powermouse*, to bombastic interpretations of European styles - like the delicious Amish Mash. You want beers with big personality? Look no further than Great Heck.

www.greatheckbrewery.co.uk 🐦 *@GreatHeckBrew*

Amish Mash

Style: **Wheat Beer/Weizen**

ABV: **4.7%**

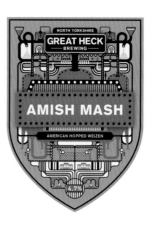

Amish Mash's aroma is all that you want a *Weizen* to be: spice-cupboard earthiness, heavy on coriander seed and white pepper, banoffee pie and a fruity smack of bubblegum. Take a sip and you'll be rewarded with subtle notes of all of the above, on top of a mellow malt base. The risingly bitter finish adds a little lime zest to proceedings, just to freshen you up before you dive in for another hit of this hazy gem. Supremely refreshing.

NORTH YORKSHIRE

GREAT HECK
— BREWING —

AMISH MASH

AMERICAN HOPPED WEIZEN

4.7%

Black Jesus

Style: **IPA**

ABV: **6.5%**

Ruby-black in hue, Black Jesus offers us another suite of heavenly aromas to get stuck into; molasses, leather, black pepper, tropical fruit and coffee all vying for attention on top of that thin tan collar. The body is full yet smooth – a distinction I find of all Great Heck's beers – packing roasted, nutty malt. Being an IPA, the finish is powerfully hoppy – all resinous pine needle and slices of mango. Enjoy with chocolate and cured meat … or perhaps, as the label says, *loaves and fishes*.

Yakima IPA

Style: **IPA**

ABV: **7.4%**

It's no idle boast of Great Heck to name this amber nectar after the famous area of Washington State that birthed the hops within; Yakima IPA is a US-inspired hophead's dream. Smooth, boiled-sweet sugars in the body of the beer provide rock-solid foundation for an aroma which sees a battle of mango, strawberry and oily, herbal pine kick off, and a finish of prickly, citrus hop leaping in. Be prepared to question the strength, too: there's only a mere whisper of alcohol on the sip.

Great Newsome Brewery

Based in Frodingham on the East Yorkshire Coast, the Hodgson family brewed their first beer on Great Newsome Farm in 2007 with a commitment to producing locally-brewed beer alongside the farming operation. Years later, the brewery is an established, award-winning outfit. The attentive Springer Spaniel that adorns the logo of Great Newsome is Jem, the family dog who roamed the brewery and, fittingly, named a stout after her when she sadly passed away in 2010. These days, visitors to the brewery will be greeted by Ruby, the new family Spaniel.

www.greatnewsomebrewery.co.uk 🐦 *@greatnewsome*

Sleck Dust

Style: **Pale Ale**

ABV: **3.8%**

To 'sleck dust' is to quench or put out a fire in old terms – or, in this case, to quench a powerful Yorkshire thirst. This graceful light ale, hopped with Centennial, Northern Brewer and Pilgrim hops, will certainly do that. It's wheaten in colour, with a cereal crunch in the body, a graceful, floral aroma and sweet finish. Expect to pour yourself a second Sleck Dust immediately after draining the first.

Frothingham Best

Style: **Bitter**

ABV: **4.3%**

A multiple award winner - the most notable being at the World Beer Awards, where it topped its category – Frotheringham Best proves that a tasty, well-brewed pint of Best still has a place in the hearts of beer drinkers. Named after the family who founded Frodingham village, this copper-red bitter with a nose of nutty, toasted malt and bright, floral finish is the steadfast backbone of Great Newsome's portfolio.

Pricky Back Otchan

Style: **Pale Ale**

ABV: **4.2%**

A "prickly backed urchin" is the rather unkind term for the humble Hedgehog in Yorkshire dialect. The beer that takes the mercurial 'hog' as its totem was only the second beer to be brewed by the Great Newsome team and remains popular today. Light amber in hue and smooth with grain in the body, the 'spikes' in this case are provided by a biting, citric finish courtesy of the Cascade hops used in the recipe.

The Great Yorkshire Brewery

The Great Yorkshire Brewery was launched in 2010 by the team behind Cropton Brewery. The Pickering brewery produces beer in cask, bottle and keg - most notably their Yorkshire Lager, which has been a huge success story not only in Yorkshire but nationwide. Now exporting to Europe and further (most notably Japan!), Great Yorkshire also produce a Cider. Look out for the neat little 'Flat Cap' lids that the bottles wear.

www.thegreatyorkshirebrewery.co.uk 🐦 *@YorkshireBeer*

Yorkshire Lager

Style: **Lager**

ABV: **4.2%**

This gold lager's aroma leans toward creamy malt, which continues through to the body of the beer, where it's joined by a touch of toffee and more light grain. These smooth, nutty notes are balanced by a zesty finish with sprightly, citric hop. Served chilled, it's perfect for barbecues and acts as a great foil for spicy, marinated meats and grilled Halloumi cheese.

Yorkshire Blackout

Style: **Porter**

ABV: **5%**

The original recipe for this stylish porter was discovered in a home-brewing log book which dated from the 1930's and found its way into the hands of the Cropton's brewer. An incredibly moreish beer, Yorkshire Blackout's aroma pushes liquorice and vanilla to the fore, whilst the beer itself is comfortably creamy to taste. Roasted grain, cappuccino coffee and more vanilla course through it, leaving a bittersweet finish on the swallow.

Hambleton Ales

Nick Stafford started Hambleton Ales in 1991, using the giant chalk white horse that's carved into the nearby Hambleton Hills as the motif for his new brewery. Nick's equine-themed beers proved so popular that expansion followed after only three years and, in 1997, *Nightmare* was crowned Champion Winter Beer of Britain. Hambleton blazed a trail for gluten-free beer in the UK, brewing *GFA* for coeliacs in 2005 and later adding a lager (*GFL*) to that range.

www.hambletonales.co.uk 🐦 *@hambletonales*

Stallion

Style: **Bitter**

ABV: **4.2**

What I love about Stallion is that although you expect a simple bitter as you pour this chestnut-coloured beer into your glass: the mix of malts used gives a lovely, creamy chocolate undertow to the overall nutty taste. The mouthfeel is full and perfectly balanced; those aforementioned malts washing over the tongue first, before being replaced by fruity, berry finish with plenty of strident bitterness.

Thoroughbred

Style: **Best Bitter**

ABV: **5%**

In 1857 Thomas Taylor carved the white horse onto the Hambleton Hills; purely because the former grocer wanted to leave his mark on the land he was born on. He and thirty strong men scored the design into the land by hand and by the time they had finished, they'd used over six tonnes of lime. They'd have appreciated this bitter's sleek flavour after completing that task – bronze in hue and packing smooth, wholemeal bread and fruit loaf flavour in the body, tempered with a hard-edged, dry citrus peel finish.

As Good As Gold

Style: **Pale Ale** (Gluten-Free)

ABV: **4.5%**

As Good as Gold is certified gluten free, and is the newest addition to Hambleton's stable of beers. Brilliant gold in colour, the nose displays plenty of toffee-apple character; hard candy and berry fruits married together. The beer itself remains sweet although the finish is certainly refreshing, especially when chilled – all lime peel and crisp, grassy bitterness. A good warm-weather guzzler, whether you're coeliac or not.

Hamelsworde Brewery

Dan Jones' Hamelsworde Brewery takes its name from the mediaeval name for Hemsworth, where he set up the brewery to build on the plaudits he had garnered throughout his homebrewing career. *Colin Brown Ale* – featured here - was awarded 'Best Strong Beer' at Doncaster Ale Festival in 2013, and rounds out the portfolio of robust, inventive beers that mix the traditional with modern tastes.

www.hamelsworde.co.uk 🐦 @Hamelsworde

Colin Brown Ale

Style: **Bitter**

ABV: **5.2%**

This beer – a gorgeous, chestnut brown bitter – is a tribute to Dan's grandfather, who was a fireman in his working days. Vine fruit and chocolate roll through the aroma (think of a Cadbury's Fruit and Nut bar), and returns in the body, supported by snappy biscuit. This punchy, bold bitter's finish is lifted by a lick of sour tartness to balance proceedings out. A complex and superbly balanced beer. Pair with sticky-sweet barbecued ribs.

Spanish Stout

Style: **Stout**

ABV: **4.2%**

It's not Spain we're referring to here but the old Yorkshire term for Liquorice – the flavour of which runs through this stout like a sticky black river. The aroma, unsurprisingly, combines gummy Pontefract cake and aniseed with a touch of woody sourness. Despite all this, the body remains light and, as you sip, intriguingly tangy cherry and port-like richness blends with complex roasted malt notes.

Harrogate Brewing Company

One of Yorkshire's newer breweries at the time of writing, Harrogate Brewery's beer all recollect local landmarks; from *Tewitt Well Ale* (which honours the ancient spa that the town is famous for) to *Kursaal Porter*, which honours The Royal Hall's heritage. Currently they only bottle one beer - which is featured here - but Harrogate Brewing Co's railway-ticket inspired livery is already a regular sight on many of Harrogate's fine bars.

www.harrogatebrewery.co.uk 🐦 *@harrogatebrewco*

Pinewoods Pale Ale

Style: **Pale Ale**

ABV: **4.4%**

Named after the woodland that sits to the west of Harrogate, Pinewoods Pale Ale is a perfect introduction to Harrogate Brewing Co's style. A bracing, modern pale ale with a lively personality, this straw-coloured summer quaffer boasts an aroma of pungent grapefruit and freshly-cut grass, which follows through to a pithy, citrus-tinged finish.

HARROGATE / 74B / PINEWOODS

SPA TOWN ALES

HARROGATE

BREWING C°

1ST CLASS
HARROGATE TO

TEWOO
LE ALE

RETURN

4.4% vol

NEW WORLD HOPS

Haworth Steam Brewery

Sitting at the top of Haworth's picturesque main street is Haworth Steam Brewery; housed in a smart, brick-and-copper clad bistro known locally as Gascoigne's. Andy Gascoigne is the man at the helm, and the brewery remains a family affair. The bistro itself is well worth a visit; serving up a wide range of continental and local specialities to accompany the lashings of Haworth Steam Beer on offer. In fact, at the time of writing, Andy was in the process of moving the brewery to a larger premises to meet demand.

www.haworthsteambrewery.co.uk 🐦 *@haworthsteam*

Austerity

Style: **Blonde**

ABV: **3.8%**

A floral, distinctly Elderflower-tinged aroma, sweet, biscuity middle and a leafy, green bitterness is what makes Austerity such a popular session beer in Haworth. As with all of Haworth Steam's beers, there's a locomotive link: The Austerity - a locomotive built in Britain, sold to Sweden in 1951 and summarily abandoned – was repatriated by members of the famous Keighley and Worth Valley Railway in 1973 back to nearby Ingrow, where it was restored over a period of years before being re-launched in 2007.

IRONCLAD 957

DARK STOUT

The Stokers Story

Our refreshing dark stout would be well deserved after back breaking work stoking the furnace. And we couldn't leave out a legend of the tracks – Ironclad No.957, this L&YR Class 25 was the original star in Haworth's famous film The Railway Children and starred in the Green Dr... 1970 gr...

Fallwood XXXX

Style: **Old Ale**

ABV: **5.2%**

This rugged, mahogany-hued brew is incredibly moreish and a perfect foil to a toothsome, sturdy cheese (Shepherd's Purse's Ryedale would be a good place to start) and sharp pickles. There's a touch of fruit in the nose cosying up alongside rich brown sugar and oak, and tart raisin and cherry notes swirling around in the body, for a balanced counterpoint of flavour.

Ironclad 957

Style: **Stout**

ABV: **4.3%**

Believe it or not, you'll be familiar with the Ironclad 957 locomotive; it was the star of the 1970 film adaptation of Edith Nesbit's The Railway Children, which was shot in and around nearby Oakworth. Pouring coal-black and mixing smooth chocolate, roasted barley and toasted bread notes with an uplifting, liquorice-accented finish, this stout would have been the perfect restorative for the loco's furnace men…or hardworking film crew!

The Hop Studio

Elvington – nestled on the banks of the river Derwent, near York – may be known for being the home of the Yorkshire Air Museum, but it's got a different kind of high-flying business to promote now: beer. Dave Shaw set up The Hop Studio there in 2012, bringing a love affair with homebrewing to a natural resolution. His sleek, classy ales have certainly found their fans across the region, particularly in York. You can't miss Hop Studio's clean branding on the bar or shelf - nor would you want to!

www.thehopstudio.com 🐦 *@Thehopstudio*

Gold

Style: **Bitter**

ABV: **4.5%**

Hop Studio's bitter pours deep amber, with a nose of caramel and pecan nut lying across brassy, bright malt. That rich cereal continues into the body of the beer, where it's joined by berry fruit, a hint of coffee, and a long, surprisingly assertive finish. Clean, refreshing and bitter – a real no-nonsense beer.

Pilsner

Style: **Lager**

ABV: **4%**

Incredibly pale when poured, Hop Studio's Pilsner will satisfy fans of the style once it's had an hour or so in the fridge. Green, flinty, mineral aroma fills the bouquet; the sip sweet and nutty, with just a hint of wheaten cereal to round proceedings out. There's a nice backwash of oaty sweetness as you swallow, before a suitably crisp finish races in to prepare you for the next sip.

XS

Style: **Strong/Old Ale**

ABV: **5.5%**

A fantastically complex bitter, XS pulls no punches in flavour or strength. With a nose that sings with deeply fruity notes of blackberry, this lusty ale pours a rich mahogany colour with a tight, tan head. Push through that and you're rewarded with bready, Dundee-cake spice, some prune and light Port flavours before the slightly tart finish cleans up. Perfect with cured meats or robust cheeses, XS is a real Winter warmer that balances flavour with alcoholic character.

Ilkley Brewery

It's hard to deny the impact of Ilkley Brewery on Yorkshire's brewing scene since their first beer (Olicana Gold) furtively appeared in 2009. Combining spa-town locality with nationwide appeal, Ilkley never seem to stop moving; always growing, always looking for the next brew to wow people with. With a beer range that runs that gamut from straight-ahead Yorkshire bitters to European-influenced Saisons and transatlantic IPA, Chris Ives and Richard Shelton's merry band of brewers remain a flagbearer for Yorkshire beer up and down the country.

www.ilkleybrewery.co.uk 🐦 *@ilkleybrewery*

Mary Jane

Style: **Pale Ale**

ABV: **3.5%**

In a remarkably short space of time, Ilkley's Mary Jane became one of Yorkshire's modern classics; a new-world influenced pale ale that drinkers can't get enough of. It's not surprising, either; the whole package screams *drink me!* Straw-pale in colour, Mary Jane packs effervescent lemon and lime sherbet into the aroma and finishes dry and long with a smattering of gooseberry. Pair that with a reference to Yorkshire's unofficial anthem *On Ilkla Moor Baht'at*, and you're onto a winner.

Siberia

Style: **Saison**

ABV: **5.9%**

Originally brewed with beer writer Melissa Cole, Siberia may have a frosty moniker but celebrates another famously fruity Yorkshire export. Fresh Yorkshire rhubarb and Vanilla are added to the beer, which come through in the flavour as a delicious sweet and sour marriage, enhanced by an earthy, woody spice note from the continental yeast that's used to ferment the beer. A refreshingly tart Saison, Siberia is wonderful – perhaps oddly – paired with rich, savoury Black Pudding.

The Mayan

Style: **Stout**

ABV: **6.5%**

This chilli stout has a dual personality; on one hand, a smooth, chocolate-led stout, all rich, *Dairy Milk* creaminess and dry, bitter roasted malt. On the other – just when you've got your tastebuds around the heart of this black beer – those chipotle chillies come roaring in, bringing punchy, fruity heat to the party. They leave a track of tingly, prickly heat across the palate, which increases as the beer dries out to a smoky finish. Supremely stimulating, The Mayan is a real conversation starter – and if you enjoyed this, check out *Holy Cow*, Ilkley's Cranberry-infused milk stout.

Imperial Brewery

Gary Sheriff has been brewing tasty beer at Mexborough's Imperial Brewery since 2011, bringing up to date a brewing career that's spanned over 20 years at the likes of Wentworth and White Rose Breweries. The brewery (now supporting a popular tap) produces cask and bottled beers for sale across all of Yorkshire and also holds popular beer festivals, which are usually a fantastic showcase for Yorkshire Beer.

🐦 *@ImperialBrewery*

FSB

Style: **Stout**

ABV: **5.6**

In this case, FSB stands for 'Fruity, Strong & Black' and I don't disagree. Much more than an exercise in strength, however, FSB carries a smoky aroma of fig, blackcurrant, sultana and roasted malt, whilst the lusciously dense adds coffee and marzipan flavours to all that fruit. The finish has a bitterness that lingers, tempered with warming alcohol.

Kelham Island Brewery

You can't talk about brewing in Sheffield without talking about Kelham Island. Dave Wickett (one of Yorkshire's beer pioneers) set up the brewery in 1990 at The Fat Cat pub in the Kelham Island area of the city. By 1999, demand for Kelham Island's beers was such that the brewery had to move to a larger location, just yards away. Now, it's the oldest operating independent brewery in the city, and has inspired many along the way.

www.kelhamislandbrewery.com 🐦 *@kelhambrewery*

Pale Rider

Style: **Pale Ale**

ABV: **5.2%**

The one that ignited Kelham Island's rise to glory. Champion Beer of Britain 2004, Pale Rider is an incredibly popular beer in both the bottle and cask. Light gold in colour and boasting a softly floral aroma recalling apricot, the familiar shortbread crunch in the body is overtaken by a gentle citrus in the finish; all lemon and grapefruit - without laying on too much bitterness.

Pride of Sheffield

Style: **Bitter**

ABV: **4%**

A no-nonsense Bitter from the Sheffield brewers; caramel-hued and packing tonnes of biscuit in the body. As the sip continues, the beer turns more bittersweet whilst  remaining softly floral, finishing with smooth toffee and a twist of tangy hop.

Kirkstall Brewery

Kirkstall Brewery, sitting on the Leeds-Liverpool Canal, is bringing brewing back to an area of Leeds that, at one time, was home not only to the original Kirkstall Brewery (which first brewed in the late 1800's), but the Cistercian monks who set up the famous Abbey, as well. Given the order's thirst for brewing, I would imagine they would heartily approve of the modern brewery's tasty wares. If you want a fresh-as-a-daisy pint, head to their nearby brewery tap, the Kirkstall Bridge Inn.

www.kirkstallbrewerycompany.com 🐦 *@KirkstallBrew*

Dissolution Extra IPA

Style: **IPA**

ABV: **6%**

A touch stronger than its cask counterpart, Dissolution Extra IPA is fantastically balanced IPA; a real blend of power and grace. Pouring burnished gold, the aroma is complex; creamy malt, a touch of peach, a hint of gingery spice and a jarful of zesty orange marmalade all compete for attention as you bring your nose to the glass. The body is thick and full-flavoured; almost honeyed with ginger biscuit. As this all subsides, long bitterness – spearheaded with more of that distinctive orange marmalade note – crashes back in, backed up by a boozy, muscular snarl of alcoholic warmth. Dissolution Extra IPA is an absolute pleasure to drink; complex and layered with flavour.

Leeds Brewery

It's hard to believe that Leeds Brewery has only been around since 2007, such is their presence in not only Leeds, but the whole county. Although their reputation is built on the amazingly popular Leeds Pale, their range of bottled beers carries the ethos of popular, easy-drinking beers that Sam Moss and Michael Brothwell had in mind when they set up Leeds's largest independent brewery.

www.leedsbrewery.co.uk 🐦 *@TheLeedsBrewery*

Midnight Bell

Style: **Dark Mild**

ABV: **4.8%**

Midnight Bell pours a rich, deep mahogany with a streak of ruby coursing through it when held to the light. The mellow aroma combines almond with subtle raisin notes, drawing you in. The sip is smooth, with a little mocha up front – which is then joined by more rich, juicy raisin and a brisk flourish of espresso coffee. *Midnight Bell* is one for late nights and cold winters: it's a warm embrace of a beer. The beer is named after the pub featured in Patrick Hamilton's novella of the same name in *"Twenty Thousand Streets Under The Sky"*.

Leeds Best

Style: **Best Bitter**

ABV: **4.3%**

This amber-hued, no-nonsense ale is one of Leeds' biggest sellers – and it's easy to understand why. Leeds Best is an incredibly satisfying pint; caramel and creamy malt dominate the body, and the dry, floral finish refreshes the palate nicely. It's a great beer to enjoy a few of with a gargantuan Sunday roast and good company. The label artwork captures the distinctive silhouettes of Leeds Town Hall and Holy Trinity Church, on Boar Lane.

Yorkshire Gold

Style: **Pale Ale**

ABV: **4%**

A piquant pale ale with tonnes of bite and a fresh, green aroma. As its moniker boasts, Yorkshire Gold pours shimmering gold in colour and piles plenty of hops onto a smooth, wheaten cereal body. As you sip, that smoothness evaporates and the finish purrs into perspective; bitter, pithy and resonating with grapefruit.

Little Valley Brewery

The roots of Little Valley Brewery stretch across continents, to a chance encounter in Nepal between Sue Cooper and brewer Wim Van Der Spek. Years later, they'd set up Little Valley Brewery, bringing Wim's extensive brewing experience to Yorkshire and mixing it with Sue's local knowledge and community spirit. As a result, the brewery – which sits on the imposing moorland around Cragg Vale – produces beers with a lovely blend of European and Yorkshire personality, as well as being Vegan-friendly and Soil Association accredited.

www.littlevalleybrewery.com 🐦 *@LittleValleyAle*

Moor Ale

Style: **Bitter**

ABV: **5.5**

This deep burgundy Ale has a complex and intriguing aroma; blending comforting biscuit malt notes with a rich, sweet smoke aspect that immediately captures your attention. Incredibly smooth in the body, there's lashings of raisin and sultana in the taste alongside bready, peaty notes. An ode to the heather-rich moorland that surrounds the brewery, Moor Ale finishes slightly tart before drying out.

Ginger Pale

Style: **Pale Ale**

ABV: **4%**

Balance is the key word here; take a crisp, cool pale ale and spike with enough fresh ginger to enhance the sharp, citrus side of the beer without going overboard. Ginger Pale's aroma sings with high, lemony freshly-sliced ginger, which reappears at the finish after gliding across crisp cereal, bringing the perfect amount of heat back into play to leave only a tingle on your lips. As fresh as a clear winter's day walk on the Pennines.

Python IPA

Style: **IPA**

ABV: **6%**

'Pale and Powerful' boasts Python's label, but there's considered restraint in this beautifully composed IPA, too. The aroma hums with fresh Pineapple and oily orange peel, which continues into the body of the beer, which is thick and sweet with malty muscle – think boozy orange marmalade and you're in the ballpark. As to be expected, the finish is long, dry and bitter with lime and lemon pith in a rolling hop attack. Despite its strength, Python IPA remains dangerously easy to drink, such is the balance on display here.

Magic Rock Brewing Co

Huddersfield's Magic Rock Brewing Co have established themselves as the clown princes of craft beer in Yorkshire since their arrival on bar-tops in 2011. Their artwork - a fraternity of freaks and circus performers - is instantly recognisable; and their beers (brewed by a team set up by Richard Burhouse and headed by ex-Kelham Island brewer Stuart Ross) are immensely popular wherever they are served, often disappearing in hours. Join the circus; you'll be glad you did.

www.magicrockbrewing.com 🐦 *@magicrockbrewco*

High Wire

Style: **Pale Ale**

ABV: **5.5%**

The cinematic, sun-blessed shores of America's West coast are evoked by this game-changing pale ale. Richly golden, the nose is all grapefruit, mango and sweet lychee – leading you into creamy malt to back up all the tropical fruit on show. The finish is briskly dry and almost juicily bitter but not raspingly so; a moreish climax to an incredibly tasty pale ale. High Wire is another one of my favourites in this guide, and is fast becoming a true 'modern classic'.

Dark Arts

Style: **Stout**

ABV: **6%**

A big beer from the big top. This strong stout boasts both flavour and aroma of blackberry, liquorice and black chocolate, tempered with a dark heart of roasted malt and rich espresso coffee. Hiding its substantial alcohol content well, this stout is hypnotic, potent and incredibly seductive. Dark Arts, indeed.

Cannonball

Style: **IPA**

ABV: **7.4**

Blazing gold when poured, Cannonball establishes that brash American IPA profile from the start: sappy, oily notes of pine and tropical fruit on the nose, rounded, smooth boiled-sweet characteristics in the body and a rousingly bitter,

rolling finish that delivers lip-smacking citrus pith in spades. The alcohol arrives later, leaving a little heat in your chest. A formidable IPA, and the base beer for even stronger versions: *Human Cannonball* (9.2% abv) and the much-lauded *Unhuman Cannonball* - which weighs in at a stonking 12% abv.

Mallinsons Brewing Co

Make no mistake; Tara Mallinson and Elaine Yendall *adore* hops. So much so that almost their entire range of beer is simply based around what hops are fresh that month. True, they also brew the odd stout, porter and bitter, but the hops are where the heart is for the Huddersfield-based duo. Mallinson's bottles are easy to spot; minimal, pastel-shaded labels with breezy, refreshingly hop-driven pale ales within.

www.drinkmallinsons.co.uk 🐦 *@Mallinsons*

Citra

Style: **Pale Ale**

ABV: **3.9%**

A showcase for the Citra hop (an American native that, as the name suggests, packs a high, pithy Citrus-peel punch), this sprightly pale ale will have you smiling in no time. First up, an aroma of peach, orange peel and tropical fruit greets you, before the smooth, gently cereal sip that provides the backdrop to all that hop personality. The finish - crisply bitter before sweetening up a little - is perfect for a low-alcohol pale ale: refreshing and dry.

Columbus

Style: **Pale Ale**

ABV: **3.9%**

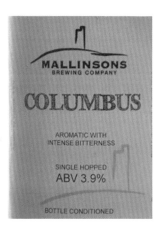

Another light, breezy pale ale at a strength that leaves you wanting more. Columbus' aroma leans more towards the green citrus of lime alongside a botanical, herbal note that carries through the pale malt and into the finish. Again, the finish is pithy, dry and long; that bitterness ramping up before fading out.

Danger Hops!

Style: **Strong Pale Ale**

ABV: **5.1%**

Straddling the no-man's land between a Strong pale ale and an IPA with ease, Danger Hops! has a thicker mouthfeel and a heftier malt profile than its pale cousins above. It's a good job too – there's plenty going on in terms of aroma, which is all freshly cut pineapple, mango and sweet tropical fruit. The finish is long and perhaps a little sharper than you'd expect from a sweeter beer – lemon sherbet and pink grapefruit dominate.

Naylor's Brewery

Stephen and Robert Naylor founded Naylor's Brewery in 2001 at The Old White Bear pub in Cross Hills (near Keighley), which they were running at the time. Realising how much fun they were having brewing beer rather than serving it, they made the leap into full-time brewing in 2006. Now, they brew a full range of cask and bottled beers under the 'Pinnacle' banner, as well as some keg beer, soft drinks – and a cider press, too. The Naylor family clearly like to keep themselves busy!

www.naylorsbrewery.co.uk 🐦 *@naylorsbrewery*

Pinnacle Blonde

Style: **Blonde**

ABV: **4.3%**

Straw-pale in colour, the tone of this beer is all about mellow, biscuity grain before it dries out, turning crisper and slightly grassy as it finishes. An easy-going Blonde that deserves to be served colder - perfect for summer drinking. Got friends who think they don't like beer and stick to lager in the warmer months? Give them this and they'll thank you later for it - fully converted!

Aire Valley Bitter

Style: **Bitter**

ABV: **3.8%**

Naylor's 'house' style, to me, is soft malt and easy-going, approachable flavours: their take on Bitter is no exception. This light, copper bitter leads with fudgy sweetness in the body, before giving way at the end of the sip and ushering in a subtle, floral finish. Perfect with cold meats, freshly baked bread and sweet, tangy chutney.

Vintage Old Ale

Style: **Old Ale**

ABV: **5.9%**

Naylor's strongest bottled beer, this complex Old Ale brings depth and a little spice to proceedings. The aroma is all Christmas cake; sultana, raisin, pecan nut and brown bread all competing for attention. These notes carry through into the body where they mingle with creamy toffee. All this sweetness is eventually tempered by brisk, ripe cherry tartness and alcohol warmth in the finish.

The Nook Brewhouse

Brother and sister duo Sheila Sutton and Ian Roberts have been carrying on the family trade in running both the Nook pub and Brewhouse in Holmfirth since 2010. An established local favourite for both the quality of its cask beer and their beer festivals, the Nook's on-site brewhouse does a roaring trade in bottled beer, too.

www.thenookbrewhouse.co.uk 🐦 *@NookBrewhouse*

Red

Style: **Bitter**

ABV: **4.5%**

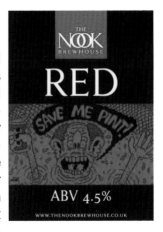

Brew a beer called Red and you'd better make sure it is – and Nook's Red passes muster. Cherry-faced when held to the light, this easy-going, sweet bitter boasts a mildly nutty body with some freshly-baked bread notes and a nose that's loaded with sticky cinder toffee. A surprisingly strident, green bitterness lifts the whole beer at the finish. Look out for a ginger-spiked version called *Fiery Red*.

Nook'y Brown

Style: **Brown Ale**

ABV: **4.9%**

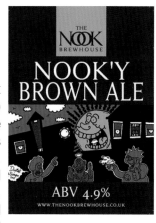

A cheeky nod to Newcastle's finest export (well, after Alan Shearer!) from the Holmfirth brewers. A true nut-brown ale, Nook'y Brown is more versatile than you first think. Light in body and – as you'd expect – deep chestnut in colour, the overall flavour is that of a swirl of caramel chocolate and toasted brown bread, with little fruity raisin laid on top.

Oat Stout

Style: **Stout**

ABV: **5.2%**

There aren't many beer styles I find as reassuring as Oatmeal Stout and Nook's is a cracker. Liquorice and bonfire toffee abound in the aroma, and the body of the beer is slick with creamy malt. Proceedings are rounded off sweetly with vanilla notes and a gentle, rolling, coffee-led finish. Oat Stout is incredibly subtle for its strength.

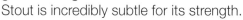

North Riding Brew Pub

Stuart and Karen Neilson are not only the hosts of the North Riding Brew Pub – a friendly, fiercely independent beer haven situated just off Scarborough's North Bay promenade – but the proud owners of their own 2 barrel brewery in the cellar, from which they provide a steady stream of tasty beer (alongside a rich tapestry of fine Yorkshire ales) to the hordes of thirsty customers who flock to the coast in search of sustenance, relaxation and a decent pint. The two beers featured here are near-permanent, but keep an eye out for the ever-changing specials brewed in-house.

http: www.northridingbrewpub.com 🐦 *@north_riding*

Neilson's Sauvin

Style: **Pale Ale**

ABV: **3.7%**

At only 3.7 per cent alcohol, Neilson's Sauvin is a delicate, spritzy treat for weary bodies after a long walk up the beach. Single-hopped with Nelson Sauvin hops (as you could have gathered from the punning name!), this almost silver-pale beer has an assertive, dry finish and a cool aroma of white grape, kiwi fruit and just a hint of peach flesh.

Peasholm Pale

Style: **Pale Ale**

ABV: **4.3%**

Scarborough's North Bay is home to Peasholm Park, an English Heritage site home to rare trees, waterfalls, Japanese pagodas and exotic greenery. *Neilson Sauvin's* bigger brother honours the name and delivers digestive biscuit malt body overlaid with green, spiky hops in the nose and finish – all citrus pith and lime jelly.

North Yorkshire Brewing Co.

Pinchinthorpe is the gateway to the Guisborough Forest Walkway as well as being the site of North Yorkshire Brewing Company, which itself resides on the grounds of Pinchinthorpe Hall. Using the famed spring waters that bubble up in the area and their own yeast strain, North Yorkshire Brewing Co produce a range of interesting bottle-conditioned beers as well as a 'custom bottle' brewing service if you want to commemorate a special occasion.

www.nybrewery.co.uk

Yorkshire Porter

Style: **Porter**

ABV: **7%**

If you're a dark chocolate obsessive, then this is the beer for you. Luxuriously smooth, this strong porter lays deeply fruity, woody, cherry and vanilla notes across a curtain of chalky dark chocolate bitterness, bringing a touch of liquorice to the nose. More roasted malt and melted Bournville notes abound in the finish, which is indulgent and smoky-bitter. The subtle thump of alcoholic heat as you sip only enhances the decadent nature of the beer.

Northern Monk Brewing Co.

Russell Bisset's Northern Monk Brewing Co began life as a "cuckoo" brewing operation in 2013. Enlisting the aid of brewer David Bishop and brewing on other people's kits, their beers were so popular that an entire re-structure of operations had to follow after only a few months to meet that demand. Now, relocated from Bradford to Leeds with a new brewing team and permanent brewery to boot, Northern Monk's smart, flavourful beers are now a regular (and welcome) sight across the bartops and beer-fridges of Yorkshire.

www.northernmonkbrewco.com 🐦 *@nmbco*

Strannik

Style: **Imperial Stout**

ABV: **9%**

As black as Rasputin's heart, Strannik is an Imperial Stout of strength and flavour. The aroma ripples with dark chocolate and toasted grain overlaid with deep, sweet blackcurrant fruit notes. The beer itself is silky-smooth, coating your tongue with indulgent mocha, tobacco and chocolate ganache flavours, before a floral, green hop note swoops in at the end to lift all that richness off the tongue. *Strannik* is Russian for 'Pilgrim', which ties in with Northern Monk's early days as brewing nomads, as well as the beer style's heritage.

Oates Brewing Co.

Halifax's Oates Brewing Company is the brainchild of Mark Oates and Richard Munro, along with brewer Anthony Barrett, who cut his teeth brewing at Surrey's famous Hog's Back Brewery. A rapidly-expanding outfit with an eye-catching set of beers under their belt, Oates' beers can be found regularly at Ripponden's Booth Wood Inn, as well as throughout the region in bottle.

www.oatesbrewing.co.uk 🐦 *@OatesBrewing*

Caragold

Style: **Golden Ale**

ABV: **4.1%**

As the name suggests, you're looking at summer in a glass here; bright gold, hazy white head and lashings of Cadbury's Crunchie on the nose, all honeycombed cinder-toffee sweetness. Luckily, the beer itself is well balanced rather than too sweet – a sprinkle of brittle, shortbread-esque malt, slices of apple and blackcurrant fruitiness, and a dash of citrus zest in the finish.

Summit IPA

Style: **IPA**

ABV: **4.5%**

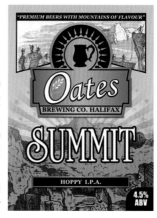

More cinder toffee pops to the surface in Summit IPA; a beer that has the initial focus on the malt bill. Sure, there's subtle hop in the aroma, which is floral and spiked with grapefruit, but the grainy, almost roasted woody malt in the heart of Summit keeps the beer quaffable and sweet. The finish is kicked along by a belligerent punch of pink grapefruit and forest fruits.

Wild Oates

Style: **Amber Ale**

ABV: **4.3%**

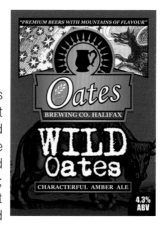

What a lovely colour Wild Oates pours – a proud, tawny amber that positively glows scarlet when held to the light. The beer itself is one for when the days are short and there's leaves on the ground; crunchy, toothsome malt that brings to mind wholemeal bread and brandy snap, a little smoke, a sprinkle of nutmeg and cinnamon, and a floral, snappy finish with plenty of residual sweetness drawing the sip out.

Ossett Brewery

Ex-Tetley's and Kelham Island brewer Bob Lawson began brewing beers under the Ossett Brewery banner in 1997 from his small plant in the back of the Brewer's Pride pub. Countless awards and expansions later, Ossett are now one of the region's most successful breweries, built on the bedrock of their super-popular pale ales *Yorkshire Blonde*, *Excelsior* and *Silver King*. As well as being an award-winning pub operator, their small family of craft breweries (The Rat Brewery, Riverhead and Fernandes) are local heroes.

www.ossett-brewery.co.uk 🐦 *@ossettbrewery*

Yorkshire Blonde

Style: **Pale Ale**

ABV: **4.5%**

With a taste as familiar as that flat-capped Yorkshire lass on the label, Ossett's best-selling beer is a real thirst-quencher all year round. Brewed slightly stronger for bottle than its 3.9% abv cask counterpart, Yorkshire Blonde is all about gentle cereal notes in the body, a generously fruity, peachy aroma and a clean, pleasantly floral finish.

Treacle Stout

Style: **Stout**

ABV: **5%**

I've personally used this beer a lot in guided tastings when discussing beer and sweets; it's fantastic with vanilla cream and red berry desserts. Pouring pitch black and brimming with black treacle, the aroma is packed with smoky hazelnut and bitter dark chocolate notes, which carry through into the body where they're joined by smooth, creamy coffee. Finishing sweet and sticky with treacle before drying out on the tongue, Treacle Stout manages to pack all this flavour in, yet remain light.

Revolutions Brewing Co.

Andy Helm and Mark Seaman formed Revolutions Brewing Co in 2010, bonding over a shared love of music. That musical theme informs every one of the Castleford-based duo's beers, giving us an endless supply of creative labels, pumpclips and beers to look out for. Initially breaking into the market with Porters and Stouts, Revolutions now brew a full range of styles to keep their fans happy.

www.revolutionsbrewing.co.uk 🐦 *@RevolutionsBrew*

Clash London Porter

Style: **Porter**

ABV: **4.5%**

It's not often that a brewery launches with a Porter, but Revolution's Clash London Porter remains their flagship; it's a chart-topper and deservedly so. Chocolate and Coffee notes abound on the nose – think of a thick smear of Nutella on burnt wholemeal toast - following through onto the sweet body where they're joined by bass notes of deep woodsmoke and a cheeky hint of sweet raisin.

Go-Go American Pale

Style: **Pale Ale**

ABV: **4.5**

You can't miss this little pink-labelled punk on the shelves! A recent addition to the rotating music festival that is Revolutions Brewing Company, this refreshing pale ale perfectly evokes the perky, sun-drenched Californian pop of The Go Go's (which launched the careers of Belinda Carlisle and Jane Wiedlin); sunrise gold and shimmering with juicy grapefruit in the aroma and a sticky, sharp lemon pith in the finish. A day-glo, rebellious power chord of a pale ale.

Manifesto

Style: **Stout**

ABV: **6%**

Manifesto Strong Stout occupies the same space as the Roxy Music album it's named after; a beer of late nights, mystery and secrets. Push through that gorgeously thick tan head and you've got a beer of subtle power; rummy, oily dark chocolate on the nose, sweet vanilla, fig pudding and roasted coffeebeans on the sip. As you swallow, bitterness increases and increases to a dry finish tinged with a warm alcohol afterglow. Fantastic.

Richmond Brewing Co.

The pretty market town of Richmond sits on the banks of the River Swale; which is only one of the local points of interest that Richmond Brewing Co use as inspiration for their softly-sweet beers, brewed with Yorkshire malt and hops grown in the UK. Set up in 2013 by Chris Wallace and Pete Loft, Richmond Brewing Co have brought beer back to Richmond, plying their trade from The Station – more of which you can find out about below.

www.richmondbrewing.co.uk 🐦 *@RichmondBrewing*

Richmond Station Ale

Style: **Bitter**

ABV: **4%**

Although trains no longer pass through it, Richmond's historic station still has plenty of visitors – it's now a community hub featuring food and drink producers, a cinema, arts and crafts and (of course), Richmond Brewing Co. This sweet-natured golden bitter packs a fruity wallop; wafer-sweet cereal overlaid with hints of cherry, plum and peach.

Stump Cross Ale

Style: **Bitter**

ABV: **4.7%**

Discovered in 1860 by miners looking for lead in the Yorkshire Dales, Stump Cross Caverns didn't prove profitable until William Newbould realised that the breath-taking, grotto-like caves would make a spectacular visitor attraction. Now it has an ale named after it too: a candy-apple red beer with an aroma heavy on malt grain; all doughy bread and toasted cereal. Again, those rich forest fruit flavours come into play as the dip disappears; raisin, a little dark, sweet cherry and plum. The lively finish is grassy and pleasantly dry, with a touch of brown sugar.

Swale Ale

Style: **Bitter**

ABV: **3.7%**

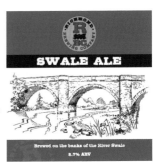

The River Swale ends its journey from the upper reaches of Yorkshire in Richmond, roaring its way through the Pennine Valley. Richmond Brewing Co's tribute - a ruddy brown ale with a complex flavour and aroma that combines earthy, crunchy malt with a touch of pear and raisin, would revive and restore hardy souls who had spent the day following the river to the brewery itself. Rich in flavour yet light in touch, Swale Ale has a crisp finish and, as a result, is incredibly moreish.

Rooster's Brewing Company

Knaresborough's finest, Rooster's Brewing Company, was set up in the early nineties by brewing pioneer Sean Franklin. He set about redefining how we think about aroma in beer with his super-pale, exotically fragrant beers. Upon retirement in 2011, he passed the reins to the Fozard family, who have since pushed Rooster's even further, adding stouts, porters, low-alcohol ales and even jasmine tea-tinged IPA's to the fold without forgetting Franklins' legacy - beers that remain in harmony between malt and hop, aroma and flavour.

www.roosters.co.uk 🐦 *@RoostersBrewCo*

Yankee

Style: **Pale Ale**

ABV: **4.3%**

This superlative pale ale is still the keystone of Rooster's portfolio of fresh, vibrant beers. Upon a backdrop of grainy, shortbread biscuit malt sits a subtle floral aroma of elderflower, citrus fruit and pine paired with a long, elegantly bittersweet finish that starts softly before drying out. A game-changing classic, Yankee helped change the market when it was introduced in 1994.

Fort Smith

Style: **IPA**

ABV: **5%**

Deep amber in colour, this IPA - named after the town in which Rooster Cogburn lived – delivers a resolutely no-nonsense hit of hops and strength. The aroma is all stone-fruit and pine resins, the honeyed and the finish sweet - before a huge Seville orange-pith bitterness rides into town and steals the show. The alcohol lingers afterward; a warming caress.

Londinium

Style: **Porter**

ABV: **5.5%**

Charged with a jolt of Taylor's of Harrogate coffee (After Dark blend, if you want to seek it out), Londinium really does put the coffee in the porter, so to speak. The nose hums with it; grainy, rich and deep, the porter's inherent woody, roasty sweetness livened by a late injection of oak and raisin before drying out completely on your tongue.

Rudgate Brewery

One of the many things York is known for is its history as a Viking stronghold, and Rudgate Brewery take their marauding legacy as their inspiration. Established in 1992, Rudgate is the name of the Roman road that ran through the airfield at Marston Moor – which eventually led the Vikings to the vale of York. Now Craig Lee's Tockwith-based brewery is one of York's favourites, with *Ruby Mild* in particular being a must-try if you see it around.

www.rudgatebrewery.co.uk 🐦 *@rudgatebrewery*

Jorvik Blonde

Style: **Blonde**

ABV: **4.6%**

Rudgate's 'flaxen' blonde ale (which is given the Viking name for York) is a huge hit in the warmer months – and it's easy to see why. The aroma brings honey-blossom and sweet malt to the fore with just a touch of grassy hop - and that caramel shortbread character appears in the body of the beer, too. It's not too sweet, though; that zippy, herbal hop finish is crisp and builds in bitterness to balance out this perennial blonde ale.

Ruby Mild

Style: **Dark Mild**

ABV: **4.4%**

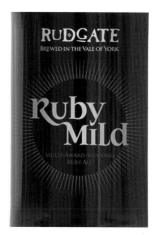

This serial award winner is a joy to sip and savour. Pouring a deep, delicious ruby, the aroma is comforting and reassuring – toffee apple, sticky toffee pudding and wheat. Hot cross bun, raisin, sweet cherry and plum all combine in the body, leaving a subtle, sweet finish to the beer that dries with touches of dense, fudgy brown sugar and fig.

York Chocolate Stout

Style: **Stout**

ABV: **5%**

York Chocolate Stout was conceived in collaboration with York Cocoa House to celebrate the inaugural York Chocolate Festival. With its roots in York's rich chocolate-producing history, York Chocolate Stout boasts vanilla and roasted dark malt on the nose, and silky, slick mouthfeel that's creamy with milk chocolate the first minute, and nuttily roasted the next. A beer that will satisfy chocoholics no end, try pairing with peanut cookies for a cheeky treat.

Saltaire Brewery

Tony Gartland set up Saltaire Brewery in 2005 with his business partners after finding the perfect location to brew in; a Victorian power station on the canalside near the world heritage village of Saltaire. Building on the commercial success of *Cascade Pale* and *Saltaire Blonde*, the brewery soon gained a cult following for their flavoured beers. Powered by a highly regarded brewing team, Saltaire remain close to their roots by hosting regular homebrewing competitions and run the region's most famous beer club, where they open their doors to beer fans for a monthly beer showcase.

www.saltairebrewery.co.uk 🐦 *@SaltaireBrewery*

Cascade Pale Ale

Style: **Pale Ale**

ABV: **4.8%**

Blending both the Cascade and Centennial (Cascade's burly cousin) hops, Cascade Pale Ale remains one of the building blocks of Saltaire's portfolio; a true modern classic. Bringing a subtle aroma of grapefruit and pine-needle to the table, backing it up with sweetness with layers of malt and then crisping things up in the finish with more sharp citrus, Cascade Pale Ale was first brewed in 2007 and was awarded Champion Premium Beer in 2010 by SIBA – the Society of Independent Brewers.

Triple Chocoholic

Style: **Stout**

ABV: **4.8%**

A blend of three dark malts and cocoa with chocolate essences makes this beer a must-try not only for chocoholics, but stout fans, too. The trick here is that all that flavour is nicely poised and balanced out; heady hazelnut chocolate dominates the nose, and the sip reveals a silkily creamy – yet light – stout vying for attention. The finish cleans the chocolate up with some green, hedgerow (courtesy of the humble Fuggle hop) notes, leading you to that next sip. A serial award-winner, Triple Chocoholic is regularly exported to America, Europe and Australasia.

Stateside IPA

Style: **IPA**

ABV: **6%**

Pouring a victorious amber, Stateside IPA was launched in early 2013 and quickly became a firm favourite amongst Saltaire's fans. The malt profile here is as big as the name suggests; sticky-smooth pulled caramel and cinder toffee, undercut with a little cake spice to add an interesting dimension. The aroma – courtesy of the blend of Cascade, Magnum, Galena and Summit hops – is everything you need from an US-inspired IPA; tropical fruit, citrus pith and oily, resinous pine which informs the bitter finish, too.

Saltaire
BREWERY
HAND CRAFTED ALES

KALA
BLACK IPA

~

CK IPA WITH SMOOTH ROAST MALT
TER AND BIG AMERICAN HOP PRES

ALC 6.2% ABV

Samuel Smith Brewery

Well, here we are: Yorkshire's oldest brewery. Since at least 1758, The Old Brewery has been turning water from that original well into some of Yorkshire's finest ales in a typically no-nonsense fashion, brewing continuously. Fermented using the "Yorkshire Square" system, Smith's ales not only have fans over here, but have found a rabid following in the United States, who can't get enough of those classic heavy bottles and ornate labelling – not to mention the pint of Yorkshire's finest within.

www.samuelsmithsbrewery.com 🐦 *@samsmithsbeer*

Pure Brewed Organic Lager

Style: **Lager**

ABV: **5%**

A classy, sleek lager. Light straw colour, the aroma is cool and floral with freshly-cut grass and cereal malt dominating. The body of Smith's lager is incredibly well-defined for such a light beer – grainy, ever-so-slightly oily pale malt sets a nutty backbone which gets sweeter as the sip continues, finishing on the soft side of crisp but thirst-quenching nonetheless.

Nut Brown Ale

Style: **Brown Ale**

ABV: **5%**

"Nut Brown Ale…" Even the name alone feels nourishing; the perfect term for a wholesome northern beer. And this famous Smith's ale fits the bill; every inch of this hazel-coloured autumnal gem whispers *comfort*. The aroma is a haze of bready yeast and, yes, nutty malt, which continues to the body where gentle shavings of milk chocolate and dried fruit come to the fore, adding depth. More nut – almond and pecan, to my taste – appears in the short, dry finish.

Oatmeal Stout

Style: **Stout**

ABV: **5%**

Reaching a perfect balance between smoky-smooth malt and tangy fruit, Oatmeal Stout pours molasses-black and wears its tight, tan collar proudly. As you lift the glass to your lips, the aroma builds with liquorice and more oily cereal underpinned by sweetly smoked dark malts. The sip is creamy yet light, bringing a little cocoa and a touch of sticky malt loaf to the table. The finish is only briefly bitter, yet rich and warming. Smith's Oatmeal Stout is perfect with Prawn Cocktail.

Scarborough Brewery

Using kit that used to belong to the now-defunct Old Foreigner Brewery in Aberdeenshire, James Soden has been brewing his well-balanced, sunny beers on the Yorkshire coast since 2010. He only started bottling in 2014, hence the single entry here, but if you want to sample their entire range, head to either the The Valley Bar or The Rivelyn Hotel – both are owned by James's family and serve as erstwhile brewery taps.

www.scarboroughbrewery.co.uk 🐦 *@Scarboroughbrew*

Citra

Style: **Pale Ale**

ABV: **4.2%**

There's not just bucketloads of Citra hops bobbing around in this beer, there's some additions of Magnum and Centennial, too. Add those onto a base of crisp pale malt you've got a zesty, pert pale ale with lime, grapefruit and a touch of tangerine in the aroma and a clean, bitter finish that becomes increasingly dry as it dies out.

Steel City Brewing

Gazza Prescott and Dave Szwejkowski (fondly known locally as "Dave Unpronounceable") set up Steel City in 2009 with one sole purpose: to brew ridiculously hoppy beer. The duo brewed as cuckoo brewers making one-off runs of (mostly) pale ales and IPA, into which they packed as many hops as they can stand. As they have no 'core range', you'll have to treat each beer you find as a special edition. Gazza left Steel City recently to set up Hopcraft Brewing in Wales, but rest assured, Dave is still shovelling hops in Sheffield.

www.steelcitybrewing.co.uk 🐦 *@steelcitybrew*

Grim Overlords

Style: **Pale Ale**

ABV: **4.9**

Brewed in collaboration with Great Heck Brewing, Grim Overlords is a classic example of Steel City's style. The uber-pale ale packs ripe peach, juicy mandarin and lemon pith in the aroma, whilst a high, cutting bitterness that's led by grapefruit and kiwi fruit slices runs through the finish. There's a little

gingery, spicy malt in the middle to round things out, but make no mistake, this is an obnoxiously hop-centric pale ale.

Summer Wine Brewing Co.

James Farran's success in homebrewing led him to "go pro" in 2008, creating Summer Wine Brewery (a nod to their Holmfirth base and the classic TV show that's filmed there) along with his partner-in-crime, Andy Baker. Over the years they've shed their image of IPA-toting hop monsters and have grown into their skin as brewers of exciting beers that blend English and American sensibility perfectly. Now orchestrating a small, incredibly dedicated team of brewers, James and Andy's 'little brewery in Honley' is now a stalwart of today's Yorkshire beer community.

www.summerwinebrewery.co.uk 🐦 *@SWBrewery*

Pacer

Style: **Pale Ale**

ABV: **4.1%**

A self-confessed *'Session IPA'*, Pacer combines low alcohol content with bags of flavour. Pouring a hazy gold, the nose brims with joyous hop – a little pineapple, some mango and a dollop of caramel sweetness. That light body is the ace in the pack here; chilled, you get a smear of honey on the palate before the whole package firms up for a crisp, citrus-led finish. Buy two of these: one won't be enough, trust me.

Mokko

Style: **Milk Stout**

ABV: **6%**

As the trio of milk cans on the label suggest, Mokko combines sweet, milky lactose with bitter roasted grain to excellent effect. The aroma leans towards the grain; roasted bitterness, a little melted chocolate and a touch of espresso coffee. The body remains light whilst introducing creamy sweetness – not dissimilar to old-fashioned milk bottle sweets – before more coffee dryness finishes the sip off.

Diablo

Style: **IPA**

ABV: **6%**

Summer Wine spent large portions of 2010 experimenting with hops and the IPA style in particular - and the outcome of all that blending and experimentation was the hellishly tasty IPA, *Diablo*. Now established as one of Summer Wine's flagship beers, it combines Citra and Chinook hops to devastating effect: sticky pineapple, mango and grapefruit in the aroma spiked with green pine; thick, honey-sweet shortbread malt in the heart, and a crashing wave of bitterness at the end that's dominated by pink grapefruit and lemon pith. For some reason (perhaps the *demonic* link in the name and artwork) I always expect this blazing amber beer to pour crimson red!

Theakston Brewery

Now firmly back under the control of the Theakston family after a period of ownership by brewing conglomerates, Theakston Brewery has now been in the brewing business since 1827. Brewing a full range of cask ales, Theakston remain part of the community in Masham, sponsoring the Nidderdale Cricket League, which is the largest village cricket league in the world. Their brewery tour and visitor centre remains popular, and they famously still employ a cooper – Jonathan Manby – who is a familiar face at food and drink festivals, demonstrating the cooper's art.

www.theakstons.co.uk 🐦 *@theakston1827*

Old Peculier

Style: **Old Ale**

ABV: **5.6%**

Note the strange spelling in the name of this famous old ale; it refers to the *Peculier of Masham*, which meant that the market town was a parish outside the control of a local diocese. There's nothing peculiar about the beer, however; a delicious, ruddy-cheeked, thick-bodied ale which tops dense fruit-cake and brown sugar flavours with a vinous, sour dried fruit notes and a leafy, bready finish - laced with just a touch of alcoholic warmth. *'OP'* is an astoundingly complex Yorkshire classic.

Timothy Taylor

One of Yorkshire's most recognisable breweries, Timothy Taylor have been brewing at Knowle Spring in Keighley for over 150 years. Using crisp Pennine water from the spring, Golden Promise malt and choice hops, their smooth, flavourful beers have a legion of loyal fans who travel from far and wide to get their hands on a fresh pint of "Timmy Taylor's" – especially cult favourites *Landlord* or the smoky, enigmatic *Ram Tam*.

www.timothytaylor.co.uk 🐦 *@timothytaylors*

Landlord

Style: **Pale Ale**

ABV: **4.3%**

A serial award-winner – including CAMRA's Champion Beer of Britain four times – Landlord sprung into life in 1952 after the brewer ran a competition to name a new beer they were designing. The steward of the Drill Hill Club in Keighley won with the simple suggestion *Landlord*, and his daughter designed the bottle label. The smiling, ruddy cheeked Landlord and his golden, fragrant beer with a firm, biscuit base and surprisingly assertive finish proved so successful that the beer was introduced in cask not long after. The rest, as they say, is history.

Havercake Ale

Style: **Pale Ale**

ABV: **4.7%**

A Havercake is an Oat cake, enjoyed and made famous by Yorkshire's 1st West Riding Regiment, whose soldiers were largely recruited from the hills and towns of the region. The beer was first brewed to celebrate their Tercentenary in 2002. A richer, sweeter beer than Landlord, Havercake Ale is robust in the body, has a sweetly fruity aroma not dissimilar to *tarte tatin* and carries an almost oily (due to the oats added in the mashing process), sticky finish of orange marmalade, which is intensely bitter. Havercake Ale is deliciously robust and as stout of heart as the men it honours. A real treat, if you can find it.

Treboom Brewery

A treboom – if you're curious – is a drumming term, and it's perfectly apt to describe the noise that Treboom Brewery have been making since they started brewing beer in late 2011. The brainchild of Jon Lewis and Jane Blackman, Treboom Brewery (who are based near York) are now bottling their bright, flavourful beers as well as making the cask ale faithful dance to their beat.

www.treboom.co.uk 🐦 *@treboombrewery*

Yorkshire Sparkle

Style: **Pale Ale**

ABV: **4%**

Cheekily billed as an RPA – a *really* pale ale – Yorkshire Sparkle is as summery a pint as the smiling sunshine on the label. Straw-hued, the nose is ripe with freshly cut grass and bitter grapefruit pith and that juicy-yet-fresh personality carries right through the light body of the beer to a racy finish that culminates with twists of lemon and lime sherbet. One to reach for when the sky is blue, the barbecue is lit, and friends are nearby.

Baron Saturday

Style: **Porter**

ABV: **5.2%**

Baron Saturday (voodoo's top-hatted, skull-faced trickster) would surely approve of this potent Yorkshire porter. It pours with an inviting tan-coloured head, with plenty of moist fruit cake in the nose. The body is thickly chewy; all molasses, currant and coffee grounds, although the finish is picked up slightly by a brisk tartness that makes you crave the next sip. A seductive, devilish porter.

Myricale

Style: **Wheat Beer**

Abv: **5%**

Originally brewed to support the Yorkshire Wildlife Trust, this refreshing wheat beer has a hidden ingredient: Bog Myrtle. Widely used in brewing before hops gained a foothold, Treboom harvest the Bog Myrtle locally and it brings a gingery, subtly woody note to the beer. With a nose that's loaded with coriander spice, lemongrass and ripe banana, Myricale is super-smooth in the body, finishing crisply with a reappearance of that fresh ginger note.

Truefitt Brewing Company

One of this guide's most northerly brewers, Matt Power set up Truefitt Brewery in 2012 after a stint brewing at Captain Cook Brewery. Taking his familys' name as inspiration – which also led to the striking, colourful jigsaw logo – he has steered Truefitt from small start-up to fledgling success in a very short space of time. If you want to get a taste for the full range, visit The Truefitt's Tap in Northallerton.

www.truefittbrewing.co.uk 🐦 *@truefittbeers*

North Riding Bitter

Style: **Bitter**

ABV: **4%**

Robust and rousingly firm in body, North Riding Bitter is one for those who think they don't like Bitter. The colour of autumn leaves, the body is rounded in flavour and recalls brown sugar and cinder toffee sweetness, capped off with a dry, roasted finish within which lurks a whisper of marzipan. A wonderfully rewarding pint.

Erimus

Style: **Pale Ale**

ABV: **3.9%**

'Erimus' is Middlesbrough's motto; it means 'We Shall Be' – and if that's not apt for a young brewery who brew beers like the ones they like to drink, I don't know what is. As yellow as the label suggests, Erimus is a honeyed, sweet pale ale with a lightly nutty body and restrained, floral finish. Pair up with grilled salmon and dill.

Truefitt Trembler

Style: **Double IPA**

ABV: **7.4%**

The hops used in this bold double IPA are a moveable feast; Matt simply uses what is fresh at the time. Which is all the more reason to seek it out when it's available; the other being that it's utterly delicious. Vibrant amber in colour, with a thick, resinous mouthfeel and a candied-fruit flavour, the aroma bursts with strawberry jam, fresh mango and crisp, herbal pine. The finish is wonderfully balanced; slowly ramping up bitterness rather than shoving it in your face – long, oily, zestily citric and then dry. A beautifully composed brute of a beer.

Two Roses Brewery

The red rose of Lancashire sits alongside Yorkshire's famous white flower on the badge of Barnsley's Two Roses Brewing – a little nod to the fact that James Taylor, the man behind the brewery, hails from Oldham. Now, fully transplanted in Yorkshire, his beers have garnered numerous plaudits in Barnsley and beyond. Two Roses brew a wide range of bottled beers; I've selected my current favourites here.

www.tworosesbrewery.co.uk 🐦 *@tworosesbrewery*

Full Nelson

Style: **Pale Ale**

ABV: **3.8%**

This thirst-quenching pale ale is a hymn to the glory of the Nelson Sauvin hop; a New Zealand native that bears an aroma of white grape and gooseberry. All those notes are present here, laid on a crisp façade of pale malt. The finish is spritzy and cool, making *Full Nelson* a very classy pale ale indeed.

Heron Porter

Style: **Porter**

ABV: **4.2%**

Heron Porter pours a rich, glossy chocolate colour and carries a hazelnut note in both the aroma and the body. There's Pontefract cake on the nose, and the smooth, sweet taste is dominated by wholemeal bread and the aforementioned hazelnut. Despite all this, the beer – as is Two Roses's signature – remains light and eminently drinkable. One to seek out if you're a porter fan.

Wall's County Town Brewery

David Wall set up Wall's County Town Brewery in 2011, building the brewery from scratch. He spent time building a local following in the pubs of Northallerton before sending his cask ales across Yorkshire and bottling when he can. Wall's beers are all bottle-conditioned, and the brewery is one of the main sponsors of Northallerton Beer Festival.

www.wallsbrewery.co.uk 🐦 *@wallsbrewery*

Beater's Choice

Style: **Bitter**

ABV: **4.6%**

Deep mahogany in colour, Beater's Choice has a cheeky personality despite the rich, chewy malt in the body of the beer. Sultana, demerara sugar and hint of almond combine in the taste at lovely counterpoint to the slightly tart finish. Nicely balancing malt sweetness and cranberry tartness, Beater's Choice is a wonderfully poised beer with plenty of depth for those who seek a little more from their bitter.

Explorer IPA

Style: **IPA**

ABV: **5%**

This amber IPA sits on the more sessionable side of India Pale Ale, but remains tartly refreshing in hop finish. The backbone of the beer leans on buttery malt whilst the aroma pulls in tangerine and orange peel. The finish is the star here, long, dry and pushing more orange-peel bitterness to the fore.

Wensleydale Brewery

Geoff Southgate and Carl Gehrman certainly take opportunities when they arise: when the pair took over the established Wensleydale Brewery in 2013 they were only in their early twenties. Age is no barrier when brewing good beer is involved, however, and they set to work cementing the existing Wensleydale range – including favourites such as *Bitter* and *Semer Water* – with new beers to reach a new audience. The Leyburn-based brewery began brewing in 2003 at The Forester's Arms in Carlton, which is now a community-owned pub.

www.wensleydalebrewery.co.uk 🐦 *@Wensleydale_Ale*

Semer Water

Style: **Pale Ale**

ABV: **4.1%**

Lake Semerwater is Yorkshire's second largest natural lake – and it hides a dark secret. According to legend, it was home to a thriving town until a beggar arrived seeking shelter on a stormy night. He was turned away from every house save one, where he stayed the night. The next day he cursed Semerwater, causing the waters to rise and flood it. The beer, you'll be happy to know, is a much happier affair; a featherweight light ale with soft lemon and lime notes on both the aroma and the finish.

Wensleydale Gold

Style: **Golden Ale**

ABV: **4.4%**

First impressions may be that Wensleydale Gold is a run-of-the-mill golden ale, but appearances can be deceiving. This burnished gold beer is packed with hops, which is evident on both the aroma – which is loaded with pineapple and kiwi fruit – and the finish, which is long, drying and sharp-edged with lemon rind and pink grapefruit.

Black Dub

Style: **Stout**

ABV: **4.4%**

Another local waterway – this time the deep, dark pool at Middleham Castle – provides inspiration for Wensleydale's popular stout. The addition of Oats in the recipe gives Black Dub a silky, almost oily bedrock on which the bitter roasted malt can sit. The aroma is bewitching; deep woodsmoke and tangy liquorice abound. A gently creamy coffee note appears in the finish to pep things up.

Wentworth Brewery

The village of Wentworth (in Rotherham) is home to the grand pile of Wentworth Woodhouse. The biggest private family house in Europe, Wentworth Woodhouse boasts no less than 21 follies, a sandstone pyramid, a 115ft tall Tuscan column and a bear pit. Most importantly (well, if you're reading this, anyway!) it houses Wentworth Brewery, which hides away in the old power station. Not only a brewer, Wentworth also bottles spring water, drawn from the reserves that sit below the estate.

www.wentworthbrewery.co.uk 🐦 *@WentworthRich*

W.P.A

Style: **Pale Ale**

ABV: **4.0%**

Affectionately known as 'Woppa' to Rotherham's beer fans, WPA (Wentworth Pale Ale) this vibrant, sunny pale ale with a golden hue and tangy, grassy aroma was the first beer produced by the brewery in the autumn of 1999. It remains a top-seller and multiple award winner amongst the South Yorkshire faithful.

Bumble Beer

Style: **Golden/Pale Ale**

ABV: **4.5%**

When Wentworth make a honey beer they really go to town: Bumble Beer contains a blend of no less than four local honeys - Lime Flower, Borage, Oilseed and Heather – and you can certainly taste it! It's incredibly rich; coating the lips with slick sweetness. Mix in a sprinkle of cereal in the body and you've got a caramel shortbread of a beer; comforting, sweet and dense.

Oyster Stout

Style: **Stout**

ABV: **4.8%**

The addition of Oysters to Wentworth's black, treacley stout gives a little mineral earthiness and salty, savoury complexity to the finish of the beer. The aroma is packed with liquorice, roasted malt and a touch of charcoal, which carries into the body where it's joined by a cherry and raisin hit of dried fruit. The savoury note appears at the end, rounded out by a pleasing tartness. An interesting and engaging stout.

Wharfe Bank Brewery

Martin Kellway's Wharfe Bank Brewery sits in an old paper mill in a quiet corner of Pool-In-Wharfedale, contently brewing robust cask and keg ales and an extensive bottled range of beer for their customers in West Yorkshire and beyond. If you want the full experience, head over to their flagship pub - The Fleece - in Otley, or enjoy a peaceful pint at their unofficial brewery tap, The Half Moon – which is a short walk from the brewery itself.

www.wharfebankbrewery.co.uk 🐦 *@wharfebank*

Yorkshire IPA

Style: **IPA**

ABV: **5.1%**

Bold malt personality and a brisk, bitter finish is the order of the day here. The aroma sings with orange jelly and tangerine skin fruitiness, backed up with that smooth, rich, body. The finish is spiked with lime zest which leaves a puckering dryness that you'd want from a modern IPA. Flashy and vibrant, Yorkshire IPA is a friend to some freshly fried fish or tempura vegetables.

WHARFE
BANK BREWERY EST. 2010

YORKSHIRE
IPA GOLDEN
INDIA PALE AL
5.1%

BREWED BY PEOPLE IN YORKS

Yorkshire SPA

Style: **Strong Pale Ale**

ABV: **5.8%**

One of only a handful of 'Strong Pale' ales being bottled in the region, SPA was first brewed in celebration of the brewery's 100th brew. A natural partner to deli meats and strong cheeses, SPA carries a subtle aroma recalling peach, which freshens up the thick, hefty mouthfeel of the beer; something to temper all that malt with. The finish is only mildly bitter, and that's where the alcohol joins the party – a warming embrace at the end of the sip.

Yorkshire Stout

Style: **Stout**

ABV: **4.5%**

Lovers of the black stuff will find nothing to complain about here: a nutty aroma, backed up by an intriguing Amaretto note, draws you near; a rich mosaic of roasted malt and dark chocolate follows. Some raisin and blackberry fruit - with a complementary swirl of vanilla - is added in the body, and the beer finishes sweetly tart before drying out completely.

Wharfedale Brewery

After buying The Albert pub in Ilkley and transforming it into a charming Dales-style inn called The Flying Duck (a reference to a previous incarnation named *The Mallard*), Stewart Ross and his team of friends promptly installed a smart brewery on-site and begun brewing simply-named, tasty beers for its thirsty customers in late 2012. Now available in bottle too, you can take a taste of Wharfedale's beer home with you.

www.wharfedalebrewery.co.uk 🐦 *@Wharfedalebeer*

Blonde

Style: **Pale Ale**

ABV: **3.9%**

A real Dales thirst-quencher, Blonde is the perfect companion to watching the summer sun set across Ilkley's renowned moorland. This simple straw-blonde ale boasts a fresh, grassy aroma, soft, slightly grainy malt in the body and a lemon-rind finish that's zingy, racy and refreshing. The finish dries quickly, which means that you're left wanting another. Better get one poured!

Best

Style: **Bitter**

ABV: **4%**

Chestnut in colour and packed with nutty, toasted malt notes, this sweet, satisfying Best is one to open on those Autumn lunchtimes when you've returned from a walk; a reviving, comforting beer that rewards the drinker with a crisp finish.

Wold Top Brewery

The Mellor Family have been brewing beer since 2003 from their idyllic farm atop the hills of Wold Newton. Over ten years later, Wold Top have grown a reputation for brewing tasty, satisfying beers including two incredibly popular Gluten-free brews. As well as that, they find time to raise money for charity, hold their own music festival at the site each year – and fill a groaning trophy cabinet of awards in the process.

www.woldtopbrewery.co.uk 🐦 *@woldtopbrewery*

Against The Grain

Style: **Pale Ale**

ABV: **4.5%**

Against The Grain has the distinction of not only being gluten-free, but incredibly tasty to boot. It's brewed with lager malt and maize, which also gives the beer an incredible silver-pale colour. This invigorating, refreshing beer is packed with lemon and lime sherbet spritziness both in the nose and the jaunty, grapefruit-accented finish.

Wold Gold

Style: **Pale Ale**

ABV: **4.8%**

Named after the undulating hills that the brewery sits on – and perhaps the golden fields that surround it – Wold Gold boasts a softly sweet aroma with hints of peach, a snappy, biscuit belly with touches of gingery spice, and a finish that begins softly sweet and creamy before developing into a green, crunchy bite. Refreshing and fulsome.

Scarborough Fair

Style: **IPA**

ABV: **6%**

Another gluten-free winner from Wold Top. Brazenly golden, Scarborough Fair is as harmonious as the titular folk song about the famous Yorkshire coastal town. A smooth, luxurious malt body is topped with a blend of three types of hop to create an oily, juicily bitter finish laden with sweet orange and lime pith. A little warmth at the end of the sip gives away the strapping alcohol content.

Angler's Reward

Style: **Bitter**

ABV: **4%**

As golden as the sun setting on a summer's day of fishing, Angler's Reward is that indeed: a reviving, refreshing bitter with a lip-smacking hop kiss at the finish – courtesy of a trans-Atlantic blend of American Cascade and UK Goldings hops. The malt used in this, and the other Wold Top beers, is grown on the Mellor's farm.

York Brewery

When York Brewery brewed their first beer in 1996, they were the first brewery to brew within York's famous walls in over 40 years. Through their quaffable, well-balanced portfolio of beers, they've slaked the thirst of many a Yorkshireman and tourist alike since. Their bottled range of beers may be small compared to their cask output, but every one's a winner.

www.york-brewery.co.uk 🐦 *@YorkBrewery*

Yorkshire Terrier

Style: **Bitter**

ABV: **4.2%**

A robust, copper-hued bitter with a lingering bitterness that nips at your heels like the vivacious little dog that it's named after. Nutty in aroma, biscuit malt flavour arrives first on the palate, which is soon chased away by that snappy, grassy hop bite at the finish. Despite being no slouch in the bitterness stakes, YT remains light on the palate.

Minster Ale

Style: **Best Bitter**

ABV: **4.2%**

Another bitter perhaps, but Minster Ale is a much zippier affair than its canine cousin, Terrier. Lighter in colour – positively gold – Minster's clean white head carries aromas bursting with orange pith and lemon zest. As you sip, the lightly cereal body is soon washed away by waves of citrus rind and spiky, bitter grapefruit. As glorious as the famous Minster itself on a clear, blue summer's day.

Centurion's Ghost

Style: **Bitter - Dark**

ABV: **5.4%**

A rich, warming beer that hides considerable strength within its dark depths. Sweet roasted hazelnut and woodsmoke fill the aroma, and these notes continue into the body where they are joined by fig, cherry and dark chocolate flavours. The finish is wonderfully poised; rousingly bitter with a little vanilla and espresso coffee, only leaving a spectral trace of alcohol. Incredibly potent, this dangerously drinkable, multi-award winning beer is not one to be taken lightly.

Yorkshire Dales Brewing Co.

Tucked away in a converted milking parlour in Askrigg – one of the little villages that dot the Yorkshire Dales – is the aptly named Yorkshire Dales Brewing Company, who have been brewing since 2005. Don't let the bucolic name fool you; and Anne Barlow-Wiltshire's beers (often named after nearby places) may include some traditional styles, but really come into their own when experimenting; Smoked porter, IPA, wheat beer, pilsner, dunkel and liquorice stouts have all found their way onto their roster in recent months.

www.yorkshiredalesbrewery.com 🐦 *@yorkshiredalesbrewer*

Garsdale Smokebox

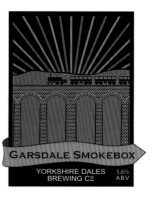

Style: **Smoked Porter**

ABV: **5.6**

That earthy-sweet smoke you can smell and taste in this beer comes courtesy of smoked malt from Bamberg, which is kilned over beechwood logs. It's the star of the show here; deep and ashy on the nose, where it's married with a little gingery spice for good measure. The sip is silky and luscious, malt tempered with raisin and a little chocolate. That smokiness flows underneath the surface of the entire beer, without overpowering any aspect of it. A real treat.

Gunnerside Gold

Style: **Golden Ale**

ABV: **4.4%**

Remember when I said to expect something a little more from the Yorkshire Dales Brewing Company? This cracking golden ale – named after Gunnerside, close to Askrigg – bears all the hallmarks of a great American pale ale: a round, sweet body packed with juicy fruit and boiled sweet notes, and a resinous, thick mouthfeel. The aroma and finish pushes those Nelson Sauvin and Challenger hops into the spotlight, all grapefruit, strawberry and a little pine. A remarkably complex beer for its strength.

Hawes Golden IPA

Style: **IPA**

ABV: **5.9%**

Imagine Gunnerside Gold taken up a notch and you've got Hawes Golden IPA. Pouring more amber than gold thanks to the blend of Munich and Vienna malts used, you've got apricot and peach on the aroma with a familiar spike of green pine, thick, chewy malt in the centre and a long, oily finish that ramps up the bitterness levels until crashing out on waves of grapefruit. Hopped with Amarillo, Herkules and Cascade hops, it's a bold, brash beer in an unassuming package.

Yorkshire Heart Brewery

A true family business, Yorkshire Heart Brewery is based in sleepy Nun Monkton, which sits between York and Harrogate. A sister project to their hugely successful Vineyard, Yorkshire Heart's traditional, appetising beers are brewed by Tim Spakouskas with input from his father Chris and wife, Gillian. The first beer was brewed in early 2011, and both the brewery and vineyard hold regular open days.

www.yorkshireheart.com 🐦 @yorshireheartbrew

JRT Best Bitter

Style: **Bitter**

ABV: **4.2%**

Hopped with Styrian Golding hops, JRT pours bronze with a leafy, floral aroma. Crisp, snappy malt dominates the body of the beer, and the mouthfeel is light and even. Only a moderate bitterness appears at the finish, giving the overall impression of a softly moreish, fragrant Best bitter.

Silverheart IPA

Style: **Pale Ale**

ABV: **4%**

The low alcohol content may sway IPA fans pursuing something a little more aggressive, but there's plenty of interest in this fragrant pale ale for those wanting a refreshing, aromatic beer for the summer. Gold in hue and packing an aroma that's biased towards citrus – peeled orange, lime and a little grapefruit – the wheaten, cereal bite of the beer quickly disappears to be replaced by a sweet finish that tidies things up with little crispness at the very end. Again, Silverheart IPA carries that lightness of body that JRT displays.

Blackheart Stout

Style: **Stout**

ABV: **4.8%**

Despite being the strongest beer of the trio here, Blackheart certainly doesn't taste it; Yorkshire Heart certainly brew with a deft hand when it comes to the weight of their beers. Blackheart's aroma is all char and roast - bringing to mind a freshly poured filter coffee – and that continues into the body where it's joined by a little dark chocolate and a hint of woody, brambly fruit. The finish is only softly bitter, which goes towards making this stout feel nourishing and comforting rather than dry and bitter.

Retailers

This guide wouldn't be much use if you couldn't get your hands on the beers contained within, would it? Here are my regular beer retailers in Yorkshire, and almost all offer great online service too – so order away!

Beer Ritz, Leeds

Beer-Ritz has been paving the way for independent beer retailing since 1988 – their shop in Headingley is my local and they have a great selection of Yorkshire beer ready and waiting for you. Check in on a weekend – local meet the brewer/sampling and tasting sessions often take place. Great staff, great beer.

www.beerritz.co.uk 🐦 *@BeerRitzByMail*

Bier Huis, Ossett

Bier Huis has been serving the beer-loving folk of Ossett and Wakefield for a few years now, putting a massive range of Yorkshire beers on their shelves alongside other local food products, Ciders and Perries.

Web: www.bierhuis.co.uk 🐦 *@bierhuis1*

Yorkshire Ales, Snaith & Malton

Adrian and Vicky Pettit set up Yorkshire Ales in Snaith in 2012 and their infectious enthusiasm for all things Yorkshire has led to runaway success – they opened a second shop in Malton in 2013. With another huge range of Yorkshire ales, wines and chutneys to choose from, they can often be found at farmers' and food markets across the region, too.

www.yorkshireales.co.uk 🐦 *@YorkshireAles*

The Hop Hideout, Sheffield

Hiding away at the back of a vintage market, The Hop Hideout is the culmination of years of supporting beer in Sheffield by locals Jules Gray and Will Linford. It's a veritable Aladdin's cave of beery treats - well worth a visit.

www.hophideout.co.uk *@HopHideout*

Beer Central, Sheffield

Beer Central is another one of the Steel city's treasure troves for local and international beer, situated in Moor Market.

@BeerCentralLtd

The House of Trembling Madness, York

Easily winning the award for "Best Name" in this retailers section, The House of Trembling Madness not only is an excellent bottle shop with a huge range of beer, but also has a neat bar upstairs. A must-visit if you're in York.

www.tremblingmadness.co.uk *@TremblingMad*

York Beer & Wine Shop, York

Long-running local beer and wine shop, with plenty of Yorkshire beers on offer as well as cheeses and cider.

www.yorkbeerandwineshop.co.uk *@YorkBeerWine*

HDM Beer Shop, Huddersfield

Another "Jack Of All Trades" retailer, the team behind Hand Drawn Monkey don't just sell bottled beer: they have an excellent microbrewery and tidy little bar, too. Pop in, buy some beer, stay for a drink and a bar snack.

www.hdmbeershop.co.uk   *@HDMBeerShop*

Beer Hawk, Harrogate

No physical store, but Beer Hawk is an online beer retailer established in early 2013. They stock a wide array of beers from around the world, putting Yorkshire classics alongside European and American imports.

www.beerhawk.co.uk   *@TheBeerHawk*

Wait a minute – this doesn't taste *quite* right….!

If you drink beer often, chances are you'll eventually come across a beer that just doesn't taste quite right. There's a few things that can cause off-flavours in beer, and I've noted the most common culprits here. To make matters slightly more complex, some of these flavours are actually desirable in small doses in certain beers but, make no mistake, when you taste a flavour in a beer that you know isn't supposed to be there, you'll know about it. Pour it away!

Diacetyl

If your beer has a really buttery taste to it, you've got a dose of Diacetyl in there. Most people say it reminds them of buttered popcorn or butterscotch, which is a good description. It occurs naturally when the beer is fermented and isn't unpleasant in small doses. It's a common fault in both cask and bottled beer and once you get a taste for it, it's easy to spot.

Oxidisation

When Oxygen gets into your beer that crisp, fragrant pale ale will soon smell and taste of wet cardboard and not much else. I always think it smells like dusty old books and can't stand it, personally. Beer should always taste fresh. Poorly fitted caps can be the source of oxygen infiltration here.

Light-strike

Mostly found in beer that's been stored in high sunlight and in clear or green bottles, light-strike produces a musky, catty

and pungently 'skunky' aroma that is simply unpleasant. Always store beer away from fluorescent light and direct sunlight.

Chlorophenols

Does your beer smell of Band-Aid plasters, TCP, burnt plastic or even taste of disinfectant? Then you've got some chlorophenols in there. It can be caused by the chlorine content in the brewer's water not being controlled correctly, or even a bacterial contamination. Confusingly, some stronger, darker beers – such as Imperial Stout - can have a similar note to them; but that's due to the grains and yeasts used in them, not infection.

Storing Beer

The way you store your beer could have an effect on how it tastes when you eventually get around to enjoying it. There's a few principles that you can follow to make sure that when you pop that cap off, the beer within is at peak condition.

- Firstly, try not to hold onto hoppier beers for too long. The brewers put a lot of effort and care into making sure that the aroma and bitterness in those IPA's and pale ales are as pure a representation of the hop as they can be, and that will simply degrade over time. Drink fresh!

- Don't store bottles on their side unless corked. In order to be effective, the cork needs to remain submerged.

- With that in mind, store bottles upright and in a cool, dark place. Obviously a cellar is the perfect environment, but if you don't have one, a cupboard away from heat sources will be absolutely fine. This way, any yeast in bottle-conditioned beers (beers that have had a little yeast and sugar added to them in order for it to re-ferment in the bottle) can settle to the bottom of the bottle.

- ...and speaking of yeast, it's really up to you as to whether you pour it into your glass with the beer or leave it in the bottle. Personally, I like to keep the yeast in Wheat and Wit beer (purely because I like the flavour), but leave it for every other style.

- Finally, stronger beers can be stored for a while to develop even more complexity. It you want to experiment with this, styles such as dubbel, stout, barley wine, old ale, imperial stout and porter are all good choices.

Serving Beer

The temperature at which you store beer has a huge effect on its flavour. If the beer is too cold – even styles like lager, which is often served ice-cold – you simply won't taste anything. Ultimately, how you like to serve your beer is down to personal taste, so I won't list a temperature range here. However, as a rough guideline:

• Lagers, IPA, Pale Ale, Golden and Blonde Ale, Wheat and Wit, Saison and Fruit beers all benefit from a little time in the fridge to chill prior to serving.

• Bitter, Stout and Porter should be served slightly cold - but certainly not chilled. Think of cellar temperature (around 11°-14° C) and you're on the right track.

• Barley wine, Old Ale, Imperial Stout and aged beer should be enjoyed just below room temperature.

The Yorkshire pint is revered across the world, a mark of quality and a guarantee of satisfaction and craftsmanship. Except there's much more to it than that – much, much more. The current boom in Craft and Microbrewing that the UK is seeing has exploded across Yorkshire, and the Yorkshire beer of today is more than just a pint of Best.

The new generation of Yorkshire brewers are breaking rules and traditions, resurrecting lost dynasties, soaking up influences from food and brewing in other countries and bringing a wave of fresh ideas to our beloved Yorkshire beer.

Leigh Linley has spent time with a handful of the region's newest and most critically–acclaimed brewers, from the south to east ridings – and Great Yorkshire Beer is their story. Each brewer is interviewed and their most successful beers are profiled. Food pairings for the beers run throughout.

www.greatnorthernbooks.co.uk